What's Wrong with America

What's Wrong with America

*Seven Challenges That Are Destroying Us
and God's Solutions to Stop Them*

FAYTON WASHINGTON

RESOURCE *Publications* · Eugene, Oregon

WHAT'S WRONG WITH AMERICA
Seven Challenges That Are Destroying Us and God's Solutions to Stop Them

Copyright © 2021 Fayton Washington. All rights reserved. Except for brief quotations in critical publications or reviews, no part of this book may be reproduced in any manner without prior written permission from the publisher. Write: Permissions, Wipf and Stock Publishers, 199 W. 8th Ave., Suite 3, Eugene, OR 97401.

Resource Publications
An Imprint of Wipf and Stock Publishers
199 W. 8th Ave., Suite 3
Eugene, OR 97401

www.wipfandstock.com

PAPERBACK ISBN: 978-1-6667-1399-2
HARDCOVER ISBN: 978-1-6667-1400-5
EBOOK ISBN: 978-1-6667-1401-2

10/14/21

Scripture quotations are from the English Standard Version Bible, © 2001 by Crossway, a publishing ministry of Good News Publishers. Used by permission. All rights reserved.

This book is dedicated to my mother. I witnessed her struggle as she dealt with the stressors of life. I knew there were many times she thought life was unfair. However, she tried to press on while carrying the weight of the world on her shoulders. I am not sure if my mother ever found peace before the Lord called her home, but I hope she knows that I will always love and cherish every moment we spent together.
Doretha Washington
6-1-1964 to 10-20-2006

This book is also dedicated to you because you are still here. You can make a change in the way you live today. Now is the time to change. Make haste, and do not wait another minute if you are dealing with any of the seven challenges that are destroying us. Life is too short for you to not live it on purpose. I offer you love and pray we all find peace and joy.
Trust God in all that you do!
Fayton Washington

Contents

Author's Note	ix
Foreword	xi
Acknowledgments	xiii
Introduction	xv
Challenge 1 | Working to Death: Your Ideal Life vs. How It Actually Is	1
Challenge 2 | Being Unhappy: Why Are We Unhappy?	22
Challenge 3 | Chasing Money: Money Never Fulfills You	59
Challenge 4 | Being Selfish: God Calls on Us to Give	68
Challenge 5 | Being Stressed: We Cannot Allow the Stressors of Life to Live Life for Us	84
Challenge 6 | Being Lazy	94
Challenge 7 | Overindulging (Sex, Drugs, and Alcohol): Everything in Moderation Is More Than Just a Saying	105
The Only Solution to the Seven Challenges We Face in America: The Only Way Forward Is through God	122
Bibliography	133

Author's Note

What's Wrong with America was written in 2016, prior to the world being exposed to COVID-19 and the devastation with which it has plagued America and the rest of civilization. Therefore, the information presented here does not consider the impact of this virus.

Also, in October 2020, the Department of Veteran Affairs finally decided to pass funding to tackle veteran homelessness, and the United States Government is beginning to address the pressures of the student loan market. However, Americans are still dying by gun violence.

Foreword

What is wrong with America? This country is currently being ravaged by so many ailments. The very fiber of our being—from the idea of instituting a democratic society to understanding what that concept truly means within the context of our interrelationships—is being threatened. It is not like we have had a blissful past; however, the transgressions of today are mounting upon each other in such rapid succession that it seems as if the earth is trembling beneath us with seismic intensity. Within its walls that span from coast to coast, under America's vast roof, and within the foundation, there are gaping cracks. These cracks are currently bursting at the seams, reeling from a common yet historic ineptitude.

Every day, the difficult task of participating in this lethargic government is too much to bear for the country's faithful. We can either stand by and watch America fall under its weight, or we can begin to rebuild and address the issues that are plaguing us.

America's obsession with the dehumanization and devaluation of life and moral principles make these cracks expand beyond mending, leading us to bear witness or actively partake in the demise of our future. This country was never going to be one flowing with milk and honey, because the land was taken by force from its indigenous people. There is no reward in that indiscretion, for the sins of our fathers may be too much to carry for such slender shoulders. Centuries later, Americans continue to be hell-bent on self-sabotage. We have been killing ourselves just to spite one another throughout America's history.

Despite dealing with the things that we cannot change, there are seven challenges we are having difficulty facing down, where we control the outcome and its impact on our livelihoods. These seven culprits deal with the fact that we contribute to our demise in preventable ways. If we can take control of our lives and alter the harmful effects these seven factors pose, we can begin living a more fulfilling life on purpose and according to God's will. The intentions of who we are supposed to be, as a people, are intertwined beyond the microscopic complexities of our differences.

Before writing this book, I had just completed reading *The Purpose Driven Life* by Rick Warren. If you have not had the opportunity to become better informed about your true purpose on earth, please avail yourself of the knowledge that is presented within its pages. It is one of the most eye-opening books about life and the true meaning of what we are supposed to be doing while we are here. Pastor Warren touches on many of the challenges covered in *What's Wrong with America,* challenges that intensify by our not aligning with God's purpose.

The seven factors tend to overlap in terms of their condition, and some of them may contribute to the onset of other factors. This combination invariably compounds the ailments with which you are struggling and that may be killing you. Many times, we tend to overlook the toll we place on ourselves and the burdens caused by our self-defeating behaviors. However, we should stop and take account of all that we do and assess how everything impacts us. We will come to realize that we are loved, have a purpose, and, above all, understand the magnitude of God's unchanging love.

Acknowledgments

Thank you to my wife for being the biggest fan and the best supporter anybody could ever ask. Also, I would like to thank my children for giving me time to write. You will always be everything to Daddy!

Introduction

The initial subtitle of this book was the *Seven Reasons We Are Killing Ourselves Prematurely and God's Solutions to Stop Them*. The book was going to be based purely on self-observations and researched statistics. However, I reconsidered the word choice of the subtitle and decided to change *Killing Ourselves* to *Challenges That Are Destroying Us* to view the issues holistically. Many of these challenges can lead to death, but it is my hope that we are able to overcome these difficulties; therefore, a title change was warranted. I consider that being overworked; being unhappy; chasing money; being selfish; living with stress; living with laziness; and overindulging flesh-filled desires like sex, drugs, and alcohol are seven vices that contribute to what is wrong with this country.

However, I figure it would be hypocritical if I pointed the finger at the struggles of others and did not offer a personal perspective regarding my struggles with some of these issues as well. Thus the book has become both a social outcry and a bit of a memoir. I have found that introspection is essential to discovering one's strengths and weaknesses. It may also help you discover whether your life is impacted by the issues discussed within these pages. Introspection may aid you in guiding others who are dealing with these issues as well. I wrote enough details about the contents of this book within the introduction just in case you are one of those people who read the intro and afterward put the book down.

This book made me realize that we all must work together to support one another. Otherwise, we live a life destined for routine societal setbacks, hurting each other in the process. For example, think about your day-to-day routine. How do you approach each day from sunrise to sunset? Many of us begrudgingly wake up to an alarm every weekday. Monday through Friday, you have this annoying sound yelling at you to get out of bed. It is not a subtle way to encourage you to wake up in a good mood, especially when you would prefer to remain in bed.

If you have young children, not only do you have a weekday alarm, but you may also awake to a human alarm on the weekend. The human alarm ensures you receive little substantial rest. Your weekend schedule can be comprised of activities like swim class, gymnastics, grocery shopping, laundry, or church. With all these activities, you are essentially working every day of the week.

As you go through your morning, perhaps you have time to eat breakfast. However, time is typically a luxury you cannot afford. You rush out of the door trying to grab your keys, wallet, and cellphone but not before you set the house alarm and adjust the thermostat. You make it to the car only to notice that you forgot your much-needed cup of coffee.

These are the day-to-day doldrums of living an ever-encompassing life that tends to move by faster and faster without waiting for you to catch up—and this is just getting out of the house in the morning. Your life is happening to you, instead of you taking charge of your life and controlling your destiny. Regardless if you are an active participant within the ongoing processes of your life, you are contributing to what happens in your life. Whether that contribution is good or bad is up to you.

Now that you are out of the house, your workweek begins. You quickly get in your car and drop the kids off at school or wait for the bus to pick them up. After sending the children on their way, you hurry to sit in traffic on your way to work (sometimes for at least an hour, depending on where you live). If you are not sitting in traffic, you are possibly riding on an overly packed public transportation system. Living in a crowded place like Washington, DC, you have probably been inappropriately close to strangers on more than one occasion. This is the hurry-up-and-wait mentality of living that so many people experience at some point in their lives.

After your listless affair with traffic in the morning, you rush to some job and work for eight to ten hours, all the while counting the minutes as they pass. By 2 p.m., you are frustratingly tired of work. You hurry to leave the job and pick up your children from school or daycare, hoping to arrive at the school before it closes. Once you are home, you are obligated to cook or prepare dinner. Then you quickly debrief each other's day and bathe the children before retiring to bed. Each of these daunting tasks is completed on day 1 of your workweek, disappointingly preparing your psyche to tackle the same set of circumstances tomorrow.

We develop a routine, with our everyday responsibilities playing themselves out repeatedly. A lot of people believe setting a routine helps to manage their busy lives. However, many of us do not realize that we are slipping into what will soon be ten, twenty, thirty, or forty years of our lives just habitually going about our days. Some of us figure out how to make at least one aspect of our routine life (i.e., raising our children, excelling at work, or being a supportive significant other) a positive experience. Other people live their lives to the best of their abilities going in and out of ruts without fully comprehending why their lives are as hard as they seem to be. The internal conflict of trying to change what you do every day, while in the throes of doing what you do every day, may be too much to bear. We become stuck, ineffective, and unable to live the lives we desire. We allow the tasks of the day to become the principle of our lives. We live to serve whatever issue we may be facing instead of living to improve our lives and seeing beyond the challenges.

We unknowingly set up goals, make aspirations, or agendas centered around supporting a lifestyle that feeds into one of these seven challenges. It is easy to see how living a mundane life or going to a job you hate can cause you to develop unhealthy habits. Working a job you loathe while trying to feed the family with whom you no longer get a chance to spend time has the propensity to make anyone unhappy. You work because you must earn a living and put food on the table. However, there is always the competition for your time (between work and family) that plagues you and causes a lot of stress.

Many people chase money, hoping it changes their situation. But the way life is set up for many of us reinforces the ideology that money alone is not the cure-all for most of life's challenges. After we are done chasing money week by week, if not day by day, we often take the same hard-earned dollars to buy materialistic items. We desire the newest this or the latest that, which allows us to show others our worldly status. Material items are not always things like clothes, cars, and jewelry. We may buy alcohol or go to a bar for entertainment.

We often get caught up spending money with the hopes of making more money on items like the lottery. Many impoverished people spend incredible amounts of money on the lottery each week. This is a behavior that speaks to the idea of using money to purchase selfish items to make us feel good about our current situation. Sometimes, this temporary act of pleasure-seeking works for a while. However, the feeling of pleasure fades and cannot be sustained for long. Usually, some new issue pops ups and that happiness you just purchased now needs a pick-me-up.

The process of chasing money and working yourself to death while being unhappy at work can cause irreparable stress in your life. Stress appears in many forms and can be derived from several factors. Stress also contributes to developing apathy, which morphs into a need to withdraw from all the things you love and care about.

Apathy can make the simple act of smiling difficult to do. Interests that used to bring euphoria may cause you to feel nothing and may even make you feel worse about your situation. You may not be able to be happy for someone's success or achievements. Apathy also tends to make you lazy, and you take your frustration out on others. You may treat the people and things you love most with a complete lack of care or compassion. Ultimately, you begin to overindulge in habits that are completely unhealthy for you in serving God and making your time here on earth really matter.

The seven topics discussed are significant contributors to the hardships we are facing in America. They also show why it is imperative to live life on purpose, since we have only the time that is available to us in this very moment to do what "thus says the Lord." We do not need to live for work, but we should work with a purpose. We do not need to live for the idea of chasing happiness, but we should seek to experience joy.

We do not need to chase money, because it will leave us every chance it gets. The Bible says chasing money is useless, like chasing the wind. We do not need to crave materialistic things. What is the point, when every materialistic thing we have will eventually crumble with the earth?

We also need to refrain from selfish ideologies and beliefs. There is no point in being selfish, when all we have acquired is tied to the fact that someone helped us along the way.

Stress needs to be understood at its root cause and dealt with at the source, so that it does not fester and cause more damage.

We must also get rid of apathy. The world needs you more than you know. It needs you to care and be productive. The next smile, touch, hug, or love that you give someone may indeed change the world. You never know how you will change that person's life or how that person will change yours.

Challenge 1

Working to Death

Your Ideal Life vs. How It Actually Is

YOUR IDEAL LIFE

The sun is shining bright on a cloudless and serene Monday morning. You can hear the chorus of melodic birds singing perfectly chimed tunes that gently massage your ear lobes as they seep through the windowpanes in the dawn. Your senses arouse your inner ambitions to thoughts of jubilation and exuberance, because today is the day you are going to excel. Today is the day you are going to exceed expectations.

The smell of crisp turkey bacon and buttermilk pancakes topped with unsalted Land O Lakes butter smothered in flavorful maple syrup conjures up the idea that the maple trees were indeed tapped directly from the backyard of Aunt Jemima's cottage. How the smell tickles your nostrils and renders you helpless to the unsatiated thoughts of devouring your breakfast! Your excitement is rising from thinking about the endless sensations your taste buds are soon to enjoy.

The morning continues to get better as you step out of bed. Your significant other kisses you gently on your lips and says, "Good morning, dear." Her voice is as soothing to your soul as the whispers of heaven's most precious angels. She goes on to say, "I have made you a lovely breakfast and look forward to making your favorite dinner as soon as you return home from work."

This must be what floating on cloud nine is like, you think to yourself. Not only has she prepared a splendid feast of which you are about to partake; she is also wearing that breathtaking red gown from Victoria's Secret. This is the exact gown she wore the night you created your firstborn. You are smiling from ear to ear, counting all the reasons she is the most amazing person you have ever known. When you glance back into the bedroom, you notice your favorite tie has been selected, along with your Hugo Boss James Sharp navy blue pindot regular fit suit. Your wife has also pulled out your favorite shirt from Joseph A. Banks. It is the one she picked up as a birthday present, with the slim fit style and cutaway collar. You again think to yourself that you are one lucky guy, and your morning could not go any better.

"Today is going to be magical," you say in the faintest whisper while reflecting on the opening sequence of your morning. Your children run to you and display tremendous love and affection. They hug you and tell you how great a father you are, and how every day they are blessed to be your children. They grab your laptop and take it downstairs for you, placing it on the kitchen counter, making it easier for you to gather your things as you leave. You did not have to bend over to tie your shoes, as the oldest child came and asked, "Daddy, can I help you with that?"

It almost feels as if it is your birthday, but that day came and went several months ago. It is now 7:30 a.m., and you have had a morning fit for a king. You are sitting in a state of disbelief, recognizing how blessed you are to be in a relationship with the woman of your dreams. She has also given birth to the most appreciative children to ever grace God's green earth. Your little four-legged buddy joins in the morning routine as he waddles across the room, wagging his little tail in admiration that he has a friend like you.

You imagine that today and every day are going to be superb. How lucky are you that your mornings come together so easily and seamlessly? Your perfect family is impeccable. There was no crying or screaming. The children got along well, and your wife cooked a lovely meal in your favorite nightie. This morning has been nothing short of a blessing.

Your trek continues as you sit in your car and turn the ignition over. The XM satellite radio station, Pandora, Spotify, or Tidal is playing soothing music as you back out of the garage, cruising along on your way to work. The benevolence of God is magnificent today. Even the lights are green, and traffic is nonexistent. How incredible do you feel, knowing you are loved? There is no rush to get to work, and the streets are as empty as if you were Tom Cruise in *Vanilla Sky*. You feel as if the world is yours, with no regrets or hesitation.

When you arrive at work, the secretary greets you pleasantly and cheerfully. The company's CEO, Mr. Johnson, calls you into his office first thing in the morning to congratulate you on how well you are performing at work and to discuss the vision they have for your career. Mr. Johnson is so excited about having you as part of the team that he offers you a raise and a promotion. You walk briskly to your office to quietly display your enthusiasm for what has transpired in Mr. Johnson's office. Then you let out a manly *yessss* while beating your chest like King Kong. It is the sort of behavior where you want to be seen, but you do not want to be a distraction. However, at that moment, you do not care who has heard your voice triumphantly echoing throughout the office, prompting some colleagues to huddle together to discover the source of the outburst. This day has been magical, and luckily for you, every day is like this spectacular occurrence. This is your perfect life—right? Wrong.

HOW YOUR LIFE ACTUALLY IS

The earlier scenario is nothing like your day. This is nothing like your life. In fact, the days of your life are the exact opposite. Your life is actually more like . . . oh, no . . . You moan, as your voice drags through the air, groggy and scratchy. "Not another day, not another day," you complain. It is that time again! Another dreadful Monday morning is here, and I tire of getting out of bed to go to this job again. I must lug myself into the bathroom and figure out how I can make this day worthwhile. I am not even sure why I am doing this to myself, you complain. If I did not have a family, I would probably quit this job right now, you internalize. Does this sound like a familiar conversation you have had with yourself a time or two? A lot of people feel some form of regret when they wake up and feel the extra pressure of Monday morning riding them to no end. This phenomenon is often called the Monday morning blues. It is especially discouraging when every morning feels like Monday morning. Unfortunately, this may be your life, and these may be your thoughts.

Every day you are confronted with the harsh realization that time is ticking by, and you are exhausted by the life you are living. You are so overwhelmed that it physically hurts. Sometimes you have aches and pains from doing nothing at all. It is not just limited to physical pain; you are experiencing emotional pain, too. The toll of living the life you have created hurts so badly you are starting to get depressed on Sunday, in anticipation of the work ahead on Monday. We cannot wait for the workweek to begin anymore before we start loathing our lives.

If this conquered attitude or feeling is true for you and most people, then why do the masses continue this unfruitful race? Is it merely for a paycheck? Is it because you were once told this is just the way life works, and you should live your life in the same manner? Or have you been doing it wrong the whole time?

In *The Ten Commandments of Working in a Hostile Environment*, Bishop T. D. Jakes writes that you will spend over half your waking life on the job.[1] The math is not too complicated, when most people typically work at least a forty-hour week. If you factor in the time it takes to get to and from work during rush hour, you may be spending at least fifty hours a week doing work-related activities. Think about spending half your waking life at work, all the while being completely miserable the entire time you are there. Does this lifestyle make any sense to you? Are you interested in spending half your life in this type of bleak existence?

IS YOUR LIFE FULL OF DOLDRUMS?

We tend to pattern our lifestyles after those who have come before us, or we do what we are taught in some form of nature vs. nurture. It takes a great deal of awareness and courage to swim upstream when everyone else is swimming downstream. For most of our lives, we were taught to get a job. It does not matter what the job was or if you had a passion for it. You just knew that you needed to get a job to survive.

Thus, people stopped thinking about their future and began to care more about making ends meet. When the bills are due and you have a family to take care of, planning for your future can seem like an unnecessary burden. I believe it is a relatively recent practice—especially for everyday people or those with fewer means—to try to figure out what their passions are. The idea of pursuing your passion was once something that only the most gifted or those who came from an affluent household could conceive as a viable option.

Now, we live in a time of entrepreneurship. This is the generation where people are starting to launch ideas and companies they care about. More people are being proactive concerning their future instead of just finding a job.

However, the practice of being an entrepreneur is still a practice that belongs to those who have a desire to pursue their passions and take a risk. Many people are afraid of taking that risk and are okay with the idea of

---

1. Bishop, *Ten Commandments of Working*, 1.

working a nine-to-five as long as their bills are paid. We are constantly searching for happiness in the workplace while feeling displaced.

Monday mornings are still the bane of our existence, and the weekend is where we seek comfort from the everyday rigmarole. It does not take long to discover that waiting until the weekend is an ineffective form of destressing, since the coveted downtime is convoluted by chores, grocery shopping, and other necessary pursuits of adulthood.

We tend to lie down Friday night only to wake up Monday morning wondering what happened to our time off from work. I am sure you have asked your colleagues after returning to work, "How was your weekend?" And the response from a few of them is sure to be "not long enough." This phrase has become more than a saying and more of an unfortunate truth. Our chemical makeup is trained by how we nurture it. If you train your mind to go through a mundane lifestyle, it will eventually succumb to this type of fragmented thinking.

The idea of living a routine life is a complicated existence that I know all too well. The notion of waking up to the same form of living and lifestyle is a lot to bear. In fact, more people die Monday mornings from a heart attack or heart disease than any other day of the week.[2] The stress of it all is probably a contributing factor.

As you grow older and mature, you begin to understand how precious life is and notice that it is solely up to you to take your life in any particular direction. However, changing directions in your life is not always something you can do on your own. There are life events that shape your future. You may be laid off or fired, someone in your family may develop an illness, you need to move to a new location, or there may be any other unforeseeable circumstance that can drastically change the course of your life.

Too many times, we get caught up living without thinking about what our next steps are, and that is when life hits us. You are left contemplating what could have gone wrong for this to be your situation. You learn quickly that the best-laid plans do not always go according to plan. As your life spirals out of control, you begin to wonder, where is your foundation for success and happiness? Which way is up? Where is your faith grounded? And how do you get a handle on your current way of life?

Understanding life's true meaning does not happen overnight, and many people believe that work is all there is to life. After all, your entire world is centered on living for tomorrow, even if you cannot see past the challenges of today. No matter how much our spiritual alignment disagrees

---

2. Miller, "Deadliest Day of the Week."

with the path we have taken in life, we somehow have found a way to convince ourselves that working to survive is the best course of action.

WORKING MYSELF TO DEATH

I can remember when I went to bed on another restless Sunday night hoping to get some valuable sleep for the usually eventful Monday morning trek. I lay in bed that unforgiving Sunday, and all I could do was toss and turn. I thought about how much I despised my place of employment; it had become more than a love/hate relationship. Sometimes you can work for a company and find some semblance of happiness either by the work you are doing or some relationships you have established at the company. Unfortunately, my disdain had become greater than any pleasantries I shared with any coworker. I asked myself questions like how did I get here? Did God want me to be here? Am I doing what God would like for me to be doing? I also thought that if I was doing what God wanted me to do, why was my heart so troubled? It felt like my heart was upset. I could feel the pressure of having to wake up the next morning and deal with the consequences of making these choices.

You probably have heard people say, "Do what you love." This phrase is supposed to be inspiring, because it is supported by the idea that if you are doing what you love, it will not feel like work. There is also the notion that you will be happier and your life will be easier, if you are doing what you love.

Well, doing what you want to do or love for a living is easier said than done for most. Many people work to feed their family or to earn some survival income; therefore, doing what they like to do may be a fantasy to them. A lot of people may be unsure of what it is they want to do or what they would consider a dream job. Brad Plumer, an economic policy journalist for the *Washington Post*, states, "Only 27 percent of college graduates have a career closely matching their degrees."[3] This stat does not bode well for the concept of chasing your passion. In many cases, it may be much more difficult to do what you want to than to do what you are currently doing. You may also feel as if your circumstances are too complicated to change jobs without the certainty of stability.

As it relates to me, I was in my career field of choice but still not doing exactly what I wanted to do. Besides, I was unhappy with my current situation and the company for which I was working.

---

3. Plumer, "Only 27 Percent of College Grads."

By the time I finally fell asleep on that restless Sunday, my alarm clock began making that repulsive sound reverberating twenty-four inches from my head. It seemed like only one hour had passed. I thought to myself that this must be what mental torture feels like. Somehow, I was able to get out of bed, clean up, and brush my teeth (which still had a minty green taste, because only a few hours had passed since I had accomplished this same task right before bed). I slowly got dressed, hauling myself through the bedroom, unsure of what I was going to wear. My wife was standing in the corner of the closet also trying to decide what she should wear, while we were both outtalking each other about the perils of our upcoming workday. Then I turned on some music to help give me a little pep in my step.

Shortly after getting myself ready to tackle the day, I had to get my children ready to go to school. It took another fifteen minutes just for them to get out of bed without crying, screaming, or completely forgetting that school was not an optional task. Kids always seem unaware that they must get ready for school on weekdays. However, on weekends, they seem to be ripping, roaring, and ready to take over the world during the same timeframe they should normally get up during the workweek. This is the irony of parenthood and it only adds to the stress of your morning.

Each morning, it is like you have an obstacle course in your home, where you are usually eliminated from the competition before you can get out of bed. Imagine being clobbered in the face and knocked into the water on *American Ninja Warrior* as soon as you start running. This is what my morning was like—absolute turmoil, with the hopes of just making it day by day, without giving up on the prospect of life getting better. My entire body and, more importantly, my mind were taxed before I stepped out of my front door, only to show up at the office and continue working myself to death.

TRAFFIC

It is hard to imagine many of us rush to catch a train or sit in traffic each morning to go to a place we do not want to be. And if we are a minute late, the train will leave us standing on the platform. However, if the train is late, there are no equivalent consequences or discounts offered for riders who may be lambasted by their supervisors due to their tardiness. Each day is a hurry-up-and-wait process.

If we had our priorities straight, the only time we would care about missing the train or rushing to go somewhere is when we were going home. Think about it, how badly do you want to be at work? However, you are expending a tremendous amount of effort to get to work and be completely flustered at your place of employment. You do not receive an award for showing up on time. It is expected of you, and rightfully so. However, when you live in a place where traffic is completely unpredictable, placing undue stress on your body and mind just to show up to work on time makes you wonder if it is all worth it in the end.

Rush hour traffic takes the cake as far as contributing to the work-until-you-die ideology. The term rush hour is completely oxymoronic, because no one is rushing anywhere, due to the sheer volume of traffic. The fact that you are sitting still on the highway invalidates the term rush. Also, if there were no traffic, would you rush to someplace you did not want to be? I can recall sitting in traffic for an hour and a half on my way to work. Then I would drive another hour to go home on the unforgiving DMV (DC, Maryland, and Virginia) Interstate 495. Cars are bumper to bumper, inching along the highway for miles.

It takes the act of positive thinking to continuously make it to the office and remain optimistic about your day. Many DC metro residents are acutely aware of how fickle traffic may be when the time difference between sitting in traffic for an hour or sitting in traffic for thirty minutes is usually a ten-minute window of opportunity. If you are later than the ten-minute mark, then you are going to be waiting for a while. But if you happen to get out ahead of the window, you may have a more enjoyable commute to work.

SENSELESS ACTS OF TRAFFIC-RELATED VIOLENCE

The truly unfortunate part of rush hour traffic is the needless cause of death related to people developing road rage. These individuals may have some repressed anger or frustration that seemingly boils over when they are on the highway. They tend to not let other cars merge, or they speed up, only to slow down 1/16 of a mile farther down the road so that another car cannot merge in front of them. Many of these people usually look extremely tired or incomprehensibly angry.

Similarly to other people, individuals with road rage may not like their place of employment either. Nevertheless, they are rushing to get to work and waste eight hours of their lives doing a job for an unappreciative employer and an undervalued paycheck. I guess if you sit in traffic long enough, you too might develop some form of road rage. However, if you ever feel rage coming on while driving, you should channel that rage and focus on what you could be doing to improve your life. Take the time and energy otherwise spent being angry to figure out how you can stop working yourself to death. Do not focus on the person who is driving alongside you, whose struggles may be similar to yours or who is painfully annoyed with traffic as well. Instead, take a moment to be kind, since you never know what is plaguing the other driver.

The AAA Foundation for Traffic Safety reports, "At least 1,500 people a year are seriously injured or killed in senseless traffic disputes."[4] The feeling of road rage is easy to understand after sitting in hours of traffic while potentially working in a toxic environment. However, before you become angry at the next slow-driving person, or before you drive too aggressively, think about what you are doing. Consider that perhaps the driver next to you is as frustrated as you are about not taking his or her career to the next level. Maybe the two of you have more in common than you think. After all, you are both just going to work or, more importantly, you both are trying to make it home.

The idea of getting to work is about as compelling as being at work. In other places, where it may be more rural, traffic is less bothersome. However, you still wrestle with the idea of having to drive to work. Your path to work is different, but your enjoyment level regarding work is the same. Overall, it does not matter where you live; getting to work can be a depressing venture that adds up to one overbearing day.

Have you had the opportunity to run to the bus, train, metro, or drive within a swell of traffic on the way to work? I am guessing most of us have had to rush to work at some point. Have you considered the type of pressure you put on your body, your mind, and your well-being just trying to make it work? Let us consider, if I were to continue the job where I was commuting by car for almost two and a half hours a day, I would be spending over two full days per month sitting in traffic. I would have literally spent a complete weekend per month just sitting in my car.

Forty-eight hours is a lot of time to miss out on being productive in any capacity of your life. Also, add in the daunting pressures of work and the idea that you are going somewhere you do not wish to be. Not only are your life's expectations not being met, but you are also not doing anything to better your outcome or position in life. How much more of your life are you going to waste being frustrated at work? Especially because, once you finally arrive at work, the real pressure is on to perform. And unfortunately for you, no matter how hard you try, some employers are never satisfied.

---

4. Montaldo, "Growing Problem of Road Rage."

THE CONTEXT OF WORK

Unless you absolutely love what you do for a living, work will undoubtedly have some good and bad days. Even if you like what you do, you will not be guaranteed to have all good days. There are many challenges and obstacles that take place during your workweek that can stymie the possibility of each day being a good day. You are also compelled to deal with different personalities that may somehow affect the feng shui of your work life. This interconnectivity between you and your colleagues can create a hostile work environment, even if you are the only person feeling the hostility. We often try to avoid becoming a Debbie Downer, the person who is always feeling negative about everything. If you are not the person who is negative, sometimes you work with him/her. This type of personality only increases your displeasure with the work you are doing.

Garland Greene, a character portrayed by actor Steve Buscemi in the 1997 movie *Con Air*, says, "What if I told you insane was working fifty hours a week in some office for fifty years at the end of which they tell you to piss off; ending up in some retirement village hoping to die before suffering the indignity of trying to make it to the toilet on time? Wouldn't you consider that to be insane?"[5] *Con Air* is a decent action film, but that statement about work and what it means to your life is a much bigger issue than the movie. However, every day, our lives are similar to what is being described as insanity. Garland was saying a lot in his soliloquy. Considering how insane his character was, he was still actually on to something.

Some people literally work most of their day without taking a lunch. Other times, people consistently work over lunch or call it a working lunch. The odd thing about this is your senior managers rarely seem to forget about lunch. They tend to go to decent restaurants, while you (if you take lunch) eat your bologna or PB&J sandwich or rush to your local fast-food establishment for some unhealthy item off the dollar menu. If this is your life, your body is slowly telling you that you are killing it. You are taking away the essence of your being by completely submitting yourself to a company that could care less if you are there or not. If the owner sells the company, you are out. If there is a layoff or a cutback, you may be out in that instance as well. The least you can do is take lunch without having to subject yourself to working during your break. It is well worth it to take a break, walk around the office or outside, and remember to eat healthy. Some employers believe in the value of breaks. Some innovative companies have put together napping lounges or exercise rooms within their facilities to help improve

---

5. West, dir., *Con Air*.

productivity and make work seem like less of an overbearing chore. But these organizations are not the norm to date.

Once, I overheard a conversation where two women were discussing their telecommuting work habits. One woman said she did not usually take lunch, or sometimes she forgets to take lunch. This woman is working from home and forgets to eat because she is so engrossed in work. By the way, her work schedule may be more taxing than commuting workers. She probably started working the moment other employees got into their cars to sit in traffic. So, the telecommuter may be working more than the normal forty-hour workweek, and she cannot seem to find the time to eat lunch. There is something wrong with those priorities and that mindset. We are so inundated with the idea of working ourselves to death that we cannot see the harm we are doing to our bodies.

As a direct response to our lives being so out of whack, an entire profession was created to free us from our daily stressors. These people are called life coaches. So now you hire a coach to monitor your busy and overworked life. As a result, you are outsourcing your well-being—and that is only if you can afford to hire a life coach. Otherwise, you must figure out how to survive within the turmoil of your cyclical life, without professional help.

IN THE OFFICE

Now you have made it through traffic and have arrived at work. What is the first thing you do when you arrive at the office? You sit in your chair, check your email, delete the messages in your voicemail, and begin reviewing the plan to get your day started. Next is your preparation for meetings or planning sessions.

The sequence of meetings is similar to the following: first, you plan to conversation points for your meeting. Then, you have your prep meeting with essential staff members. Shortly after the preparation meeting, you have the actual meeting with people who barely remembered the objectives from the previous meeting. These unprepared colleagues are the reason you go over the details of last week's meeting before you begin this week's meeting. Finally, you meet to discuss the actual data points and takeaways from the meeting after the actual meeting. You have already had four meetings today, and that was just your morning.

The time spent in meetings is sometimes your biggest waste of time. Those meetings may have also caused you to work over your lunch, now that most of your day was spent in session. According to TED Talk speakers David Grady and Jason Fried, "There are more than three billion meetings every year, with executives spending forty to fifty percent of their total working hours in meetings. Almost thirty-four percent of all meetings end up as wasted time, which indicates that executives are flat-out wasting almost eight hours of their workweek—nearly a full day of work every week." That is a lot of time spent looking at your colleagues' faces. Not only is the time lost, but there is also a loss in productivity that will only add to your work stress later. Grady found that the loss in productivity is estimated to waste nearly $37 billion every year in the US alone.[6] Not only do meetings take up your time, but you loathe them as well. The rest of the day you are overtasked with goals that should be completed in conjunction with at least another staff member or two. Nonetheless, you are left to complete the tasks by yourself, because your company is understaffed.

If you are performing physical or manual labor, your job is a little more interesting. Perhaps you stand in the sun for eight to ten hours as a construction worker, drive for days on end as a truck driver, produce products, or construct some object for months or years until the task is completed. Unfortunately, the worst part is that a lot of employers are not interested in showing appreciation for the effort you exhibit for the betterment of the company. You are simply just another body that the company could replace if it needed to. This is what your workday is like for at least five consecutive days. All the while, we continue to ask ourselves, "Is there a better way?"

AT HOME

The previously belabored description of work speaks to the paid portion of your work life; however, the other facets of your life are just as stressful and time-consuming. For example, you rush home to make it in time to pick up your children from daycare, school, or some other activity that states you should be in attendance with haste. If you are a parent, you may have to cook dinner, entertain your children, and review their schoolwork. You should also show some love to reassure your children that you care and that you are not just going through the motions.

In your lifetime, taking care of your children is the most important thing you will likely do. Young children typically require a little more of your attention than work does. Although you do not spend as many awake hours with your children, the impact you leave on their lives has the potential to weigh more than any product or service you can produce or sell.

Your evening routine consists of feeding them dinner after it has been prepared, remaining on suicide watch (making sure they do not kill

---

6. See references in Pidgeon, "Economic Impact of Bad Meetings."

themselves or each other), and bathing the children before you tuck them into bed. Before you know it, your body is completely exhausted, your mind is taxed to its furthest extent, and you literally have no more energy to give to your day or yourself. If you have a significant other, then there are other responsibilities of companionship in which you may indulge before you can go to sleep. Hopefully, you can muster up five to six hours of sleep before doing it all over again.

This is not a healthy lifestyle, since you do not have any recovery time or any time for yourself. You are sleep deprived, which can lead to hypertension, diabetes, obesity, depression, heart attack, and stroke. There is so much pressure in your life that adding one more thing may cause you to break.

Are you satisfied with this existence? Is this the life you want to live? Do you think about the time being spent in an existence that is not anywhere near what you want to accomplish? If going to work, being at work, being in the wrong environment, hating your boss, or disliking your employees captures your feelings about work, then you need a change. That mindset completely drains you. Think of all the hours spent riding on the metro or sitting in traffic alongside everyone else with the most miserable look on their faces as well. They are probably looking back at you, seeing the same thing in your demeanor. It is difficult to be happy when you are surrounded by things that make you unhappy.

This lifestyle is commonly referred to as running the rat race. However, we may be giving the rat a bad reputation, since the rat will receive some cheese once his wheel stops spinning. What do you have to show for your tireless effort? A zero to minuscule income increase, decreased value of life, and unbalanced work-life equation. The worst part is that you may have to work past your desired retirement age to live comfortably. Actual retirement ages vary greatly across socioeconomic statuses; therefore, some of us may have to work much longer than others.

Employers no longer have to offer guaranteed pensions and can now offer a 401k plan to their employees. However, government-backed retirement plans have their limitations and are really a tool for the middle class to remain middle class. I could continue, but this is not a money management book. In any case, I can recall sitting in employee benefits meetings for one of my previous employers. The CEO was never present during any of the 401k meetings. I knew the CEO well and was aware he was going to retire soon. Why wouldn't these meetings be relevant to him but were relevant to the staff? I later learned that there are other tools that wealthy people use for retirement—and they are not 401ks.

There are better vehicles to help you retire; however, those retirement tools are not readily available to the masses. Also, the stock market is untrustworthy, especially for laymen; yet more than 50 percent of Americans have their retirement savings invested in one or more types of index-related financial instruments. I have relatives who worked all their lives and had their money saved for retirement, only for the market to crash. They ended up losing everything and had to continue working to try to make up what they had lost. Making sure you are properly preparing for retirement only compounds your problems. Along with not having enough money when you retire, there are other factors like being unappreciated, not being happy for at least ten hours a day, and missing out on your purpose, all of which may weigh heavily on your heart.

MY WORK-LIFE JOURNEY

I once worked for an employer where I was tasked with being the lead marketing director. I was making a six-figure salary (like I prayed for) and had decent benefits. I was living the dream, and my life was completely what I told God I had wanted as a little child. The 1997 movie *Soul Food* had a character played by Mel Jackson who was a marketing director, and his salary was $80,000 per year. These were goals. And as the biblical saying goes, ask and it shall be given to you. When you develop a relationship with God, he tends to do what you ask if it aligns with his will. Thinking of life through my lowly human mind, I thought those material goals would make me happy.

I later realized that God had provided all my earthly desires at a young age. I had set goals for myself when I was a kid growing up in Blakely (Salters), SC, without much in the way of material value. Now I had a wife, kids, cars, a house, and a six-figure salary. I had thought that I would have to work so hard and be a much older man by the time I had accomplished those goals. At least I had thought I would be in my mid-forties by the time all my goals came to fruition.

However, these were the goals of a young child and were far too simple for God. First Corinthians 13:11 states, "When I was a child, I spoke like a child, I thought like a child, I reasoned like a child. When I became a man, I gave up childish ways." Those were childish ambitions, and God had bigger plans for me. But I did not realize that at the time. God made my childhood dreams come true at the age of thirty-two. How shortsighted was I to dream so small, when God had so much more in store for me! And the most incredible thing is that his goals are not financially based.

I made it my mission to get things done at my place of employment and tried to improve how their current operations were going—at least I thought I was offering improvements. I took it upon myself to delve deep into the company. I developed new programs, created marketing plans, and changed some existing processes that were not performing as well as they could have. I despised the idea that this company felt great about breaking even on most of their events. To me, in business, breaking even on all your events does not make sense. I believe if your company is not growing, then your company is dying. I helped the organization host its largest and most important meeting ever during my time there. This was at a time when they were having trouble getting customers to attend. I also helped clients gain a better perspective of the organization and obtain more value from the company. I came home and worked on other tasks for the company when I should have been spending more time with my family.

I ran the rat race and became seriously vested in the future of the organization. Regardless of my efforts and contributions, I never received a thank you from my direct supervisor, who was the president and CEO at the time. It felt like the work I performed was not appreciated by direct leadership. Other leaders and co-workers did praise the changes and urged me to continue to help the organization move forward. Nevertheless, when it came time for the company to make changes, I was let go. As a result, it was the very thing I found pleasure in doing—and on which I had centered my childhood dreams—that was provided as part of the reason for my being let go. I was told my salary was too high, and I brought an entrepreneurial style to a traditional company. My direct supervisor mentioned, "You will land someplace where your entrepreneurial style will be better suited."

Silly me, believing that bringing an entrepreneurial approach to an employer was a good thing. I was initially taken aback, because I had contributed a great deal of work and time to help the organization advance its mission. However, in the end, that did not matter.

On my last day, as I was leaving the company, one of the senior staff members stated, "You had an impossible job." He said, "It was just completely impossible."

So, you run this rat race to have it all come to an end before you run through the tape. I was initially disappointed, because I had a young family to feed. I was faced with having to go home and tell my wife that these dreams I had cherished as a child were crushed. I guess 1 Corinthians 13:11 was right; it was time to start thinking like a man.

The CEO also added, "This decision was not personal." Perhaps it was not personal to him, but it was very personal to me, because my family would be directly impacted. It was as about as personal as it can get. Luckily, my wife was employed with a well-paying job of her own and was supportive during my time of trouble. I recall talking with her on the phone while waiting at the metro stop. She told me that she loved me and everything was going to be okay. It was comforting to hear her say those words, although it did not feel like everything was going to be okay. I could not get the words "I love you" out of my mouth in reply, because I was standing there trying not to let tears fall from my eyes while being choked up, wondering how I was going to fix this problem. Again, just another story of someone who had to understand what God had in store for him, who had to learn not to invest your all in your secular work. We all must realize that our lives are so much more than our nine-to-five.

KAROSHI

Every day you go about completing your responsibilities, trying to please your boss and do well by your employer, only to face the realization that you may be let go in a downsizing, staff disagreement, or acquisition. Is it worth it, when you look back at the time spent? Should you find something that makes you feel better about the type of work you are doing? Is there something more for you to do while you are here on earth?

Many people work or feel the need to have any job. But is this job completing you or just helping you to make ends meet? Are you fatigued and dissatisfied with the path your life has taken? Some people live this life every day. Perhaps, more commonly, this dissatisfaction with life is the norm.

I can only imagine the stress that single parents are under while trying to hold it all together. Consider the amount of pressure with which they may be dealing—perhaps having to deal with more than one child under the age of ten—while working a job or two. One can assume that managing work and life is stripping people of their true purpose, especially when working is all that they do.

The Japanese have coined the term Karoshi, whose literal meaning is death from overwork. An article by Kary Oberbrunner notes that the International Labour Organization defines Karoshi as a sociomedical term that refers to fatalities or associated work disability due to cardiovascular attacks (such as brain strokes, myocardial infarction, or acute cardiac failure) aggravated by heavy workloads and long working hours.[7] This is the exact definition of your life being centered around your job. It takes precedence over everything else, and, in return, you die from Karoshi. According to an article in Reuters, Japanese workers had a record-high number of 1,456 claims for death due to Karoshi in 2015.[8] I believe our numbers may be close

---

7. Oberbrunner, "Six Warning Signs."
8. White, "Death by Overwork."

to that of the Japanese, as Americans work for longer hours than those in most other countries do.

Oberbrunner relates the Karoshi phenomenon to long work hours, heavy workloads, lack of job control, routine and repetitive tasks, interpersonal conflicts, inadequate rewards, employment insecurity, and organizational problems, all contributors to this unfortunate way to die.[9] Americans deal with a similar subset of problems as we face these mounting challenges at work. The stress alone can become unbearable. The article goes on to discuss that burnout (34 percent of respondents think they will burn out in two years), heart attacks (33 percent increase), injuries (25 percent increase in work-related injuries on Monday), death (more people die at nine o'clock Monday), and suicide (male suicides are the highest on Sunday nights) are contributing factors to Karoshi as well.

When people reference that they receive only four to five hours of sleep or become adept at not sleeping at all due to being plugged in, they are unfortunately on the path to Karoshi. We need to work on getting ourselves out of this rut and change our lives for the better. However, the ability to connect to work is omnipresent with the advancement of technology.

It is difficult to not allow work to interfere with your mental mindset. Leaving work at work is no longer an effective solution when access to work is available 24/7. This is in part due to the mobile world in which we live. Exchanging late-night emails, early morning calls, or texts make it exceedingly difficult for you to pull away and understand what it is that you would like to do with your life. It becomes difficult to focus on things that matter most. What was once your forty-hour workweek has ballooned to a fifty- or sixty-hour workweek, and it is difficult to know when or how to stop working. Ponder the amount of stress and angst you feel as you spend more time away from your well-being or your family. You must find time to align the right balance in your life.

Do you want to continue this lifestyle? When do you pull away to refocus on what is profoundly important to you?

It is important to take a vacation. But for most people that is not the answer. Vacations usually require more work for parents. Some people work full-time and cannot afford the time off to take a vacation, or they do not have enough money saved up to take a vacation. Therefore, they are stuck trying to utilize weekends for leisure time. Unfortunately, the weekend is also filled with chores and other responsibilities.

---

9. Oberbrunner, "Six Warning Signs."

So, when do you begin to align your purpose and the work you do with the mission that God has for you? When do you stop falling victim to Karoshi? Maybe it is time you start to figure it out.

FIGURING IT OUT

So how do you define God's purpose for your life? That is the question, right? You need to figure out what the next steps are, so that you are not continuously working for the sake of working. Psalm 127:2 says, "It is in vain that you rise up early and go late to rest, eating the bread of anxious toil; for he gives to his beloved sleep." We are not supposed to skip the rest we so desperately need. Work should not stymie our body's need to rest. Instead, we should work with a purpose that will satisfy our souls and be pleasing to God while obtaining an appropriate amount of sleep.

There is a concept emphasizing the idea of living on purpose. This notion is designed to help you live a more fulfilling life by following the desires of your heart, which should align with the direction God has set for your unique journey. I urge you to make time to engage in the book *The Purpose Driven Life* by Pastor Warren. I believe it will aid you in understanding who you are and what you should be doing while you are here on earth. Pastor Warren writes, "You were made by God and for God, and until you understand that life will never make sense."[10]

I believe once we accept this belief and start living according to this simple principle, life will change, and we will no longer be working ourselves to death. You will not go home after a day at the office feeling like you have just sinned. You will begin to understand what drives you internally and develop clarity around your circumstances, knowing money is not the answer. Money only satisfies the materialistic aspirations of the world, and those aspirations are short-term. You will soon tire of the clothes you wear. You will soon tire of the car you drive, or perhaps the car will break down at some point. The stock market will suddenly crash, and you may lose some of your money. These things are inevitable, and if you are working to satisfy these needs, you may be missing the point of living life on purpose. Bills become larger, and pressure becomes more intense the more your monies increase. Therefore, money cannot be the driving factor behind your desire to solve the working to death problem. Your purpose is much bigger than that.

As previously mentioned, during my teenage years, I discussed with God my desire to acquire a two-story house (my mother's dream), a beautiful and loving wife, at least two kids, and a six-figure salary. I genuinely

---

10. Warren, *Purpose Driven Life*, 21.

thought that was all I needed in life. I believed that once I accomplished those goals, I would have it made. Little did I know, my ambitions would continue to increase, and the aspirations of a young boy would not be my life's work. What do you do when God has already surpassed your childhood dreams?

My dreams started to change when I realized that the dreams were those of a child and not of God. God's dreams for me are much more than I could ever imagine. His purpose for my life was not fulfilled by the dreams I had set as a child. It felt like he stated, "Is this all, my son?" It felt as if he shared those thoughts with me while continuing to impress upon me the following notion of "now that I have given what you asked, I have a purpose and a mission for you to accomplish."

The weight of God's words is magnified throughout your spirit when his mission for your life is shared with you. In fact, we all have a mission to accomplish. I still receive a tug at my spirit every day that I am being pressured by man or by my earthly desires. It feels as if my actions are in direct conflict with the path God wants me to travel. He has already surpassed what I could ask for, and the basic necessities in my life have been attained. Now he wants me (like he wants you) to pursue my purpose. So back to the question, how do you discover God's purpose? How do you continue?

You continue by taking the time to think about what God has for you. He has already told you what he wants you to do. He probably showed you your purpose when you were in grade school, sitting in traffic, or during your daily life. I heard a pastor say that God does not waste your past, so consider every experience when exploring your purpose. Perhaps it happened when you helped someone. It may have been when you prayed to him or just by happenstance.

However, so many of us decide not to do what God has asked or decide to put God's purpose on hold, as I did. Once you combine what God wants for you with that spirit-filled tugging at your passion, you will know what work you are truly supposed to be doing. It may be that you are currently working where you need to be in this season.

God structures your life to make you better, if you continue to pursue his will. Even if what you are doing is not currently where God ultimately wants you to be, do your best and work as if you are working for God. It is all part of God's plan. You need to discover the driving factors at your current company that allow you to grow spiritually. Explore the assets that will enhance your spirit's awakening as you contribute to the company's bottom line.

Your work life does not have to be a one-way street. Align all you do with the desires of God, and you will begin to experience the joys that overworking has hidden from you. You can even pray sincerely about the issues you are facing at work and watch God begin to move in your favor. The more you develop a relationship with God, the more you will see that he is there. He is listening to the issues that plague you. He will fuel your passions.

Once you have figured out what is feeding your passion and connect that passion to the desire God has for your life, you will be on a path to victory. You will no longer be on a path of working yourself to death but working with a purpose. You will also be living with a purpose and not existing within the confines of breathing but existing within the constructs of God's agenda for your life. You will work with the idea of knowing you are contributing to what God has placed in your heart for the betterment of yourself and the glorification of his kingdom. Your family will also reap the benefits of your newfound direction. Your life and the work you are doing will start to make sense. It may take some time to figure it out, but when God asks you to move, do so with haste. The time we have here on earth is limited. Therefore, once you are aware of what God has ordained you to do, pursue it with undeniable faith.

We must take the necessary steps to change our desire of being hell-bent on killing ourselves at work. Your desire should develop into a quest of discovery, trying to understand how to get right with God. Then, everything will begin to line up correctly. You will feel less pressure in your work environment, because you are working with a purpose. Your frustrations will turn into understanding. Suddenly, the people at the office who normally bother you—be it supervisors or employees—will no longer be able to get under your skin.

THE CHANGE

Why does this change take place? It is because you have become aware that there is a purpose in what you are doing? As you change, even traffic may not bother you as much. The time you spend in traffic could be used more productively when you channel your energies to God and work on your relationship with him as you creep along the highway. Instead of being frustrated by traffic, you may rejoice in the life you are living. You will also start making other things in your life a priority, like your children and your relationships with others.

These changes will become the impenetrable walls that will protect your heart and guard your relationship with God. When undesirable things happen at work or around you, your wall will be there to protect you and ensure that you are well taken care of. You will be aware if a godless presence is in your life or if your relationship with God is becoming a bit strained. Working to death will become a thing of the past, and working on purpose will be your destiny. God only wants us to surrender ourselves fully to him. We will gain a better understanding of who God is and how he moves within us.

You should feel free to question God on anything you do not understand while you are developing your relationship with him. There are numerous stories in the Bible, including stories about Jesus himself, where God's purpose for the individual's life was questioned. People no longer understood how God was moving within their world. Jesus asked why he was forsaken, and Job wanted to know what he did wrong to receive his harsh treatment. Be empowered to ask God questions about work and what it is you are supposed to do in this life. Watch him open the flood gates of initiative, drive, and understanding.

However, remember the devil listens to your prayers as well and will fight to keep you going down the wrong path. As I have learned from Pastor Stephen Chandler of Destiny Church, these are called distractions. They are put in place to distract you from God's purpose. To break the chain, you must remain in faith and move according to God's plan. Once you begin working on your relationship with God, working to death will no longer be a challenge you have to face, since God's love will help you overcome and be all you need.

Challenge 2

Being Unhappy

Why Are We Unhappy?

Work can be attributed to people not being happy with their lives. Susan Adams, an author at Forbes magazine, quotes a study by the Conference Board (a New York-based nonprofit research group) that states that 52.3 percent of Americans are unhappy at work.[1] However, work is only one factor. Being unhappy has more to do with you as a person than just work alone.

Marketwatch.com writer Quentin Fottrell wrote an article discussing five reasons Americans are unhappy.[2] The article's subtitle is "Why People Living in One of the Wealthiest Countries in the World Are Glum." This speaks to the idea that money does not bring happiness. One rarely has to do with the other.

Fottrell's first reason we are unhappy is the theory that we are zoning out with gadgets, thus missing our emotional connections. I agree technology is completely incapacitating our ability to connect emotionally. The internet is filled with content that graphically displays our inhumanity. Instead of helping one another, we are recording and posting brutal fights or disagreements between people. These are the videos that receive incredibly high viewership, competing with the cutest video of a cat sitting on a couch in a stupor. Images such as these contribute to why we are not seeing the

---

1. Adams, "Most Americans Are Unhappy."
2. Fottrell, "Five Reasons Americans Are Unhappy."

great things that make us all interconnected. Instead, we are communicating by technology, while missing the best parts of being human. His second point of unhappiness reflects the fact that 50 percent of people say they are stressed out, which we will discuss in detail in the next section. Stress may be the underlying agitator for many unhappy people. It is caused by many factors. Therefore, understanding the causes of your stressors is the most important step to finding your happiness again.

Fottrell's third reason is following the lifestyles of the rich and famous. We are dooming ourselves because of the need to chase money and be like the Joneses. However, we are completely unaware of the struggles the Joneses face behind closed doors. We are better situated in life if we define life in terms of what will make us most satisfied and pleasing to God, instead of chasing the materialistic rewards of the world. The Joneses are humans living with the stressors of life just like you.

Fottrell's fourth reason we are unhappy is our lack of siestas in the US. I think this one is hilarious, because, as much as America believes it is the best country, we treat our citizens like America is one of the worst countries. You would think that America had a formula for success; however, we are no longer the economic force we once were. Sure, we have the highest GDP and largest economy, but at what cost to the sanity of the workers in this country? European countries whose currencies, schools, and livelihoods are better than ours also offer a better work/life balance than America.

We must be doing something wrong here at home. All our positive economic indicators are not able to assure us of happiness or help us understand why America's citizens are so unhappy. We know we are overworked, but what else is contributing to this country's unhappiness? What is contributing to your unhappiness?

Fottrell's last point indicates that most Americans are unhealthy. Later I discuss our tendency to be lazy, as well as our perpetual behaviors that lead to overindulging in terrible behaviors like poor food choices. Each of these habits leads to Americans being unhealthy—so he may be on to something.

Fottrell's article offers these few reasons as to why we are unhappy. The reasons we are unhappy are worth considering, because the result of being unhappy can be devastating and sometimes lead to premature death. Dying is not the only thing you have to worry about as an unhappy person. You may also become distant from the people and things about which you care most, thus negatively impacting those you love while you wallow in your sadness.

DEPRESSION

If unhappiness lingers, it can turn into depression. A DSM-IV criterion for Major Depressive Disorder (MDD) is expressed as a depressed mood or a loss of interest or pleasure in daily activities for more than two weeks.[3]

This explains why it is necessary to address unhappiness before it escalates into depression. Brandi Koskie added an article on Healthline.com that reports that depression affects one in ten Americans.[4] It also mentions that states with a higher number of people with depression have high rates of obesity, heart disease, stroke, sleep disorders, lack of education, and less access to medical insurance. The report states a combination of societal and self-care issues that presents as commonalities with depression may contribute to unhappiness.

Discovering your reasons for unhappiness is pivotal to helping you discover what happiness means to you. First, happiness is nothing more than a feeling of euphoric bliss. It is an emotion that is tied to a sensation we feel due to some varied stimulus. It is not a permanent state of being, and it does not last very long. There is a time limit on happiness, because, as you live, your emotions will change due to changes in your environment, your circumstances, or even the weather. Therefore, your happiness should not be tied to material things, societal issues at large, or emotions. And you should not look for happiness in other people, as this will often end in a failed endeavor.

LOOKING FOR HAPPINESS IN OTHER THINGS

Many people are trying to find the key to happiness. They look for happiness in fickle relationships or in other people. You may have crossed a woman or two saying if they had a good man, that would make them happy and they would be complete. Men have often thought that money equals happiness. Some men believe the more money they have or the more they can buy, the happier they will be. However, we are fools for even considering that having a man or having more money will make us happy. In this regard, one plus one does not equal two. We will not find true happiness in another person or with more money. You may be happy for a short period, but this attachment to happiness will not last. The excitement or novelty of a new relationship will fill you up and make you think you are on cloud nine. However,

---

3. National Institute of Mental Health, "Major Depression."
4. Koskie, "Depression: Facts, Statistics, and You."

when your money runs low or your relationship takes a turn for the worse, happiness tends to bail on you right along with that situation.

Alanna Petroff, a writer for *CNN Money*, writes that the financial crisis of 2008 contributed to thousands of suicides. Petroff says, "New research published in the *British Medical Journal* showed the impact of the crisis led to nearly 5,000 additional suicides in 2009 compared to the norm. Nearly the entire increase can be attributed to men taking their own lives, according to the survey of data from fifty-four countries. In the U.S. and Canada, male suicides jumped by nearly 9 percent in 2009."[5]

These dreadful statistics indicate that you should not predicate your life, and the joys of life, on the expectation of worldly things. Your life is more valuable than the money you make. It is more valuable than the job you have. All these things will bring temporary happiness and then take that happiness away, just as fast. Unfortunately, the individuals who killed themselves during the financial crisis erroneously chased money right to the end. This is an unhealthy relationship with money, and it is one that can never be satisfied.

THE EMOTION OF HAPPINESS

Happiness wraps itself in nice clothing and shows up from time to time, but it is never there to stay. A simple point of reference could be related to America's infatuation with sports. This week, your favorite football team bests its rival by twenty points. You are excited and happy for the week now that you have bragging rights. All your friends will suffer through your gloating about how well your team played, consequently bringing you loads of happiness. Sadly, this feeling of exuberance will last for only a week, because the following week, you may witness your team lose to the worst team in the league. Now the happiness with which you were so full a week ago is replaced by feelings of bitterness. Again, this is a simplistic way of looking at how fleeting the emotion of happiness truly is.

But this ideology can spread to your family as well. Think of your child doing well in school or performing well in a play or some athletic activity, only to come home and have a temper tantrum or speak to you in a disrespectful manner. You react both positively and negatively to both incidents, allowing emotions to control the outcome. You are elated one moment and filled with anger the next. This is the problem with happiness being considered an ideal mental state.

---

5. Petroff, "Financial Crisis Caused 5000 Suicides."

HAPPINESS IN RELATIONSHIPS

Emotions are always irrational, and true happiness should not be tied to them. Otherwise, you will experience an ebb and flow of happiness. A married couple who builds their relationship on happiness will go through this emotional ebb and flow often. If they are not laughing and playing all the time, they may not know how to interact with each other. They may be unaware of their significant other's complete character traits if happiness is all they see. What happens to the relationship when one person becomes unhappy? What happens when they experience a tough situation, where the emotion of happiness is not available to the couple? For example, what happens when someone loses a job and financial turmoil creeps into the relationship? What happens when someone is depressed or stricken with a terminal illness? What happens when you have an escalated argument? Happiness forsakes us all at some point. What do you do when happiness forsakes you?

When I talk to people who are about to get married, I always say two things. First, do not go to bed mad at each other. This is followed by always sleep in the same bed. You should never be comfortable sleeping without your significant other. Second, make sure you argue before you get married. You may never argue after marriage (which is highly unlikely), but when two people are coming together, their personality differences sometimes clash. You need to learn how to deal with each other positively, even when you are at odds with each other.

These two principles are not based on happiness. They are based on love overcoming anything that happiness may not cover. Happiness is not something on which to solely build a relationship, since it is weak and flailing, like all emotions are. Many people may have said they are not happy in a marriage and immediately look to a divorce for the answer. However, this is not the answer. Malachi 2:15–16 states, "Did [the Lord] not make [the married couple] one, with a portion of the Spirit in their union? And what was the one God seeking? Godly offspring. So guard yourselves in your spirit, and let none of you be faithless to the wife of your youth." Yet, when trouble arises, we run to the courthouse ready to end our relationship, although we said before God that this relationship is what we want.

Happiness is fleeting; love is eternal. Your relationships need to be stronger than emotions. The instability of being happy is why being unhappy is so easy to fall into. We should seek happiness within ourselves and from the grace of God first; then everything else will fall into place. However, if we truly seek God, he will offer us more than happiness.

FEELING UNWANTED BY YOUR PEERS

The world can sometimes be a harsh place to live. Many people are vain by nature. We tend to judge everything by what we see or what we have been taught and less on intellectual curiosity, love, and trust. Many people are criticized by how they look or what they possess instead of who they are and the content of their character, to paraphrase Dr. King. We are a country of segregation and separation. From the start of our interactions with people as an adult, we labeled and characterized others based on their perceived value. What is their value to us, and what do they bring to our lives? We are taught to view each other in this narrow manner instead of accepting one another as we all are—humans. Think of all the hate-filled clashes that have plagued America recently. Many of these are a result of feeling unwanted or unwelcomed.

FEELING UNWANTED IN AMERICA

America is supposed to be a country of people with differing thoughts and ideologies who operate collectively for the greater good of this county. However, what we seem to do best is cause other factions of people to feel like they are outcasts or less than another segment of people within this multiracial country.

During the 2016 presidential election, Republican presidential nominee Donald Trump did a great job of making people feel less welcome in this country. It seemed as if he discriminated against the entire Muslim religion and the Hispanic community. This type of behavior has the potential to cause an entire religion and race of people to feel ill will toward America. These feelings may come upon them, regardless if they are citizens or not. If you are a citizen but consider yourself to belong to one of these factions of people, you may develop a feeling of being unwanted in your own country. African Americans have had a long-standing history of feeling unwanted in America. Many minorities feel they are at odds with the country they call home, the place they were born, or the location to which they migrated to better their situation. As the largest Christian country in the world, America is supposed to be a beacon to all nations showing what an open and welcoming society should look like. Lately, it has been anything but open. Careless politics, oppression, unacceptable anger, and ill-conceived ideologies are the key ingredients to developing a country of intolerance.

UNWANTED CHILDREN

Adults tend to develop an understanding of people directly through the idea of judging a book by its cover. It is not often that adults veer out of their comfort zone when it comes to accepting someone who has a different background or upbringing. Work is one place where we are forced into that dynamic, but, if left to their own devices, people seldom develop relationships outside of their bubble. These are missed opportunities to develop a relationship with someone who may be experiencing loneliness or feelings of being unwanted right there at work.

Children are exposed to a feeling of being unwanted or different at a young age. From kindergarten through college, children separate into groups of the cool and not cool, and then you have the people who do not care about fitting in at all. It is sort of a survival instinct to identify yourself by the beliefs of other people with whom you share similarities. Children start little cliques or group together with friends. Depending on the alpha of the group, they may take on the personality of that individual. The groups begin to grow into people who are not just hanging out but into individuals who are alienating other children. Sometimes, these groups make fun of others who may be perceived as different, which could be something as asinine as tattered clothes, disheveled hair, being too big, being too small, wearing glasses, having braces, or anything of the sort.

This behavior creates a feeling of being unwanted or not belonging. A child's mind is fragile, and if it is broken at a young age, it may continue to be broken throughout her life. This child unwanted by peers may develop feelings of initially being unhappy. Without a stable source of refuge, the child can eventually lash out at those who make her feel inferior. Hopefully, she will find somewhere to turn and not retaliate because she was labeled as different by someone whose opinion does not matter in the grand scheme of life. Children can be mean to each other. It takes a strong and aware parent to be there if his or her child is the one being labeled as an outcast.

Many children begin to become bullies or are being bullied themselves due to perceived feelings of being unwanted. Between one in four and one in three US students say they have been bullied at school, according to Stopbullying.gov, a government platform dedicated to ending bullying of all kinds.[6] Most bullying happens in middle school, and the most common types are verbal and social bullying. Kids are learning to treat others differently and begin to develop feelings of being unwanted at impressionable

---

6. Stopbullying.gov, "Effects of Bullying."

ages. Stopbullying.gov validates that point, stating that young people who are perceived as different from their peers are often at risk for being bullied.

It is up to us, as parents, to step in and support our children if they are being bullied. If your child is the one who is bullying other children, it is your responsibility to correct this behavior before the bullied children lash out or your child's bullying behavior becomes worse. It is up to you to teach that being different is not wrong. Being different is what makes us all special, and bullying or treating someone badly because you have differences is wrong. A report by ABC News found "nearly 30 percent of students were either bullies or victims of bullying, and 160,000 kids stay home from school every day because of the fear of bullying."[7] This mistreatment of one another has to stop, simply because it typically leads to future harm. According to the Centers for Disease Control and Prevention (CDC), youth who report both bullying others and being bullied (bully victims) have the highest risk for suicide-related behavior of any groups who report involvement in bullying.[8]

There is also a separation of who looks pretty and who does not. Who is smart, and who is not? Who is athletic, and who is not? Who is dating this person or spreading rumors about someone else? The separation never ends, and we continue to find ways not to like one another or to make someone else feel unwanted. How often do we stop and think that something as vain as beauty is a gift from God and is in the eyes of the beholder? Yet we allow meaningless traits like beauty and appearance to define how we treat someone.

Being unwanted may cause you to develop feelings of unhappiness. That unhappiness can lead to a self-defeating way of thinking, if it is not addressed at an early stage. Lack of exposure and understanding of other people create this idea of pitting people against one another.

Like children, we separate ourselves into groups of people or classifications to form unhealthy communal opinions. Although there should be no more judgments among us, we have religious groups boycotting homosexual weddings and funerals, religious sectors continuing to war across the world, and others judging how someone loves God. Yes, the Bible has its stance on homosexuality, but, above all, the Bible says to love, forgive, and do not judge one another—even our enemies. There are also the rich hating and stealing from the poor, the poor stealing from one another, parents killing their children, and children killing their parents within America. We

7. Bullying Statistics, "Bullying and Suicide."

8. Centers for Disease Control and Prevention, "Relationship between Bullying and Suicide."

are creating this world of carelessness for one another. We are not supporting, forgiving, or accepting, thus leading to people feeling unwanted and unhappy.

THE BIBLE'S THOUGHTS ON YOUR DIFFERENCES

My wife and I make it a priority to introduce our children to a variety of people. They have friends of all shades of colors and ethnicities. At the current ages of five and two, they do not have any indication of race or separation. All they see are people. The most they understand about color is as much as Crayola has shown them in a box. At some point, we will teach them how America identifies them. But this identification is the creation of a separatist mindset that pushes us from one another.

Americans have a habit of teaching our children that, because we look this way or someone else looks another way, we are different, thus creating reasons to separate ourselves. The divide only continues from there, until someone is left out and feeling unwanted, which compounds their unhappiness. Psalm 139:14 says, "I praise you, for I am fearfully and wonderfully made. Wonderful are your works; my soul knows it very well." This verse explains that you should not feel unwanted, because God made you. When we consider all the things that are different about people of the world, take the time to think about how many more things we have in common.

Isaiah 43:4 offers support by stating, "Because you are precious in my eyes, and honored, and I love you, I give men in return for you, peoples in exchange for your life." If all else fails and you get to a point where you do not feel wanted, know that God wants you. He desires you, for you are his child. Do not let the opinions of another get you down or make you feel unwanted, because God has shown you favor every day. God wants you as you are, no matter how different people perceive you to be. Sacrifices of both a biblical and physical nature have been made for you, when you consider the people who died for your freedom or rights. We are here to show appreciation, forgiveness, and love for one another—not to dwell on insignificant differences.

UNHAPPINESS IN RELATIONSHIPS

We place a lot of stock in our relationships. These relationships tend to make or break us each time. As a result, our happiness suffers along with the relationship. Hopefully, we can go into each relationship and obtain something valuable from it as we journey through life. Perhaps we can learn a little about ourselves and a little about someone else. Relationships come in a variety of forms and can consist of family, friends, or coworkers. However, personal relationships, the ones we hold near and dear to our hearts, are the ones that tend to take a toll on you and your health.

These are the relationships where you have invested the most amount of time and energy. You can extend yourself in a personal relationship without reciprocation. The practice of giving your all in a relationship is oftentimes unhealthy for you and directly impacts your well-being. The strain of trying to hold something as delicate as a relationship together by yourself is difficult to do. Relationships must have balance.

Our relationships are vital to extending our lives here on earth. Pastor Warren states in *The Purpose Driven Life*, "The second purpose as to why we are here is to be a part of God's family."[9] This means we are all God's children and that establishing relationships with each other is important to our existence. Think about adopted children who may not know their birth mother. Although she did not play any role in the child's upbringing, there is some biological connection that makes the child long to know its birth mother. We should have this same connection to one another; we should desire to know one another, as we are all family in the eyes of God. We are all brothers and sisters, and we should revere each other as such.

The strains in our relationships are without a doubt one of the biggest issues with which we are dealing in America. We do not know each other, and we do not care to get to know one another. How much can you grieve for someone with whom you do not have a connection? This lack of relationship explains how we can kill each other and not think about the greater impact. We have lost the urge to connect and the longing to know more about someone else. We have lost the ability to care.

As spiritual brothers and sisters, our compassion should pour out if something happens to a family member. But we have strayed so far from one another that we have become less of a family and more like strangers. This country has always had a relationship problem, and this problem will surely destroy the fabric of our being if we do not correct it.

BROKEN RACE RELATIONS

America's race relations problem is one that is unbearable to watch. People still are loathing each other because of the color of another person's skin. I

9. Warren, *Purpose Driven Life*, 117.

have met people with characteristics of which I am fond and some of which I am not so fond, with varying degrees of racial differences and ethnicities. As my wife and I joke, we practice equal opportunity prejudice behaviors. It does not matter if you are Caucasian, African, Hispanic, Asian, or any other ethnicity of American, your character makes you who you are. If you are a hateful person, we will take note of that. If you are a loving and kind person, we will take you for who you are. Your race has nothing to do with your character.

America still breeds people who think they are better than someone else because of the color of their skin. White people hating black people and black people hating white people are not only stereotypical ideologies of America, but, as the saying goes, it is as American as a hotdog. However, these are unfounded prejudices. And just like a hotdog, this hatred is full of things that are not good for you. We are all children of God, and we will be judged the same no matter the color of our skin. The crimes, shootings, riots, and politics of race have to come to an end, as this is one of America's greatest wrongs.

WHERE TO LEARN ABOUT RELATIONSHIPS IN THE BIBLE

Believe it or not, many of America's problems exist because we have a relationship problem. Pastor Warren points out that the Ten Commandments are all about relationships. Each commandment focuses on our relationship with God and our relationships with each other. We have broken every commandment, because the structures of our relationships are in ruins.

First Corinthians 13:13 also offers a solution to our relationship problem. We must get through the hate to realize our solution comes from the following verse: "So now now faith, hope, and love abide, these three; but the greatest of these is love."

We must instill love and extend it to each other. There is no other way for peace to exist without hate being eradicated. We must remove this unbridled desire to kill each other with reckless abandon. We are dying at a rapid pace just dealing with the onslaught of natural disasters. Many areas around the world are suffering through once-in-a-lifetime flooding travesties, wildfires, mudslides, hurricanes, tornadoes, and global pandemics. At the rate of earthly retribution, Mother Nature will prove her point to us all soon enough. Therefore, instead of killing each other, we need to develop better relationships with each other and grow closer together in love.

MY RELATIONSHIP WITH GOD

In addition to improving our relationships with one another, the most important relationship we must cultivate is the one we have with God. If we start by simply developing an understanding of what it means to love God, we can begin to learn how to love each other. Even though our relationship with God is the best relationship for us to have, this relationship can be a tumultuous one. Look no further than Job for an example that sometimes even a relationship with God can be one that challenges you.

As a young child, I found myself falling in and out of a relationship with God. However, I desperately needed this relationship when many of my closest relatives passed away. I also needed this relationship when I would feel lost. There would be moments when I could feel how close God was to me and other moments when I could tell how distant I was from him. I searched and longed to have a relationship with God. I went through the process of being saved three times, thinking that just saying those words, despite not having true conviction, meant some miraculous change would take place within my life. I guess I thought God would have mercy on me, although I was not willing to completely change or advance my faith. I thought that if I backslid from God's mercies time and again, I should go and get saved each time. It was not until this moment that I realized that people backslide all the time. I came to recognize that it is not God who changes or moves away from us, but it is we who change. We are the ones who damage our relationship with God.

I have had some interesting otherworldly experiences in my life that made me reflect on my relationship with God. I can remember as a child receiving high marks on a writing assignment in elementary school. I came home and showed it off to my mother. I was proud of my accomplishment that day. I was so pleased that I hung it up on my wall with a flathead white pushpin. I went to bed feeling rather good about the grade I received. Later that night while I was sound asleep, I heard someone or something in the dark speak in a possessive tone say "This ain't **it" and rip the paper off my wall. The paper drifted slowly, swaying back and forth until it hit the floor. I awakened the next morning thinking that what occurred last night was a dream. However, as I opened my eyes, I saw the paper lying on the floor torn from the pushpin that was still affixed to the wall. I also noticed a small laceration on my back. I understand that this may sound a little like an episode of *Unsolved Mystery* or some movie about a haunted house in Connecticut. But at the time I believed this was some battle between good and evil or some sort of spiritual warfare. It was a blatant reminder that with every good thing, there may be some bad.

After going through something like that, I figured the time was right to develop a relationship with God. I am not saying this was a demon or some exorcist event that occurred; however, it was real enough for me to begin developing a relationship with Jesus. Also, it was not the last time I had an unexplainable scratch on my back appear out of seemingly nowhere. It made me a little timid to discuss these incidents with my wife until she saw it for herself once. Believe me, it is hard to explain random scratches on your back to your wife.

These incidents made me question my relationship with God. Life was going easy for me and I was not facing any adversity, so I thought these scratches were lessons in humility. Were these incidents happening because I was trying to get closer to God? Or were they scratches that showed up randomly? I have learned to always be leery of the easy path, since God never said your journey would be easy.

The closer my relationship grew with God, the more I could feel the world fighting for me to remain within its realm of sin. It is not always an outward battle. Many times, the battle to follow God or to do what you want in the way of the world is an internal struggle. That is why this relationship is one that must be worked on and endured. I have never once heard God say a word to me or heard his voice, but I have felt his presence or have been shown things at the right time based on a conversation I have had with God. His presence is not always a pleasant feeling. Sometimes, the closer you get to God, the more you can feel him rebuking you for the sinful things you do. God's relationship is one of faith. I can admit my relationship with God can be stronger and more perfect. But I know without a doubt he is with me, just like he is with you, helping along the way. Seek to develop your relationship with God, and watch him intervene.

PICK EACH OTHER UP

Galatians 6:2 states, "Bear one another's burdens, and so fulfill the law of Christ." God carries our burdens every day, and we should be willing to lend a hand to one another similarly to how he helps us. Let us share each other's burdens of being Caucasian American, African American, Hispanic American, Asian American, Muslim American, a single mother, a woman, a fatherless child, rich, poor, sick, or just human.

If we carried each other's burden, we would learn to connect more and pick each other up when something goes awry. We need to focus on love and doing what "thus says the LORD" to ensure our relationships are exactly as he wants them to be—filled with love. We can love each other beyond worldly love, where someone gets hurt because they did not cater to your feelings. But if we can genuinely love each other and support one another the way God loves and supports us, the rest will take care of itself.

UNHAPPINESS WITH FAMILY AND FRIENDS

Family, friends, children, parents, and especially significant others are foundational relationships that if not cultivated and treated properly can take a toll on your health. Many of these relationships are supposed to strengthen you, and they should be at least a 50/50 partnership. Apart from the parent-child relationship, all others should be created equal. A parent should be willing to give his or her all to the upbringing of the children and raise them as God would want them to be raised. This relationship is unequal until the point where a child can reciprocate. Even at the precipice of the relationship's maturation, the parent should remain the comforter and the guider of truth. Except for a parental relationship, many other types of relationships should resemble equality.

However, relationships are rarely structured this way. Oftentimes they are parsed as percentages of 70-30, 80-20, or 100-0. The individual who is receiving less but giving more is the one who will be negatively impacted the most. The other individual is rarely there or may be unaware of the fact that he or she is not contributing to the relationship in any meaningful way.

Think about your situation. Do you have a family member or friend who is always in need of something from you? Do you have a family member who is always in trouble, in need of money, or some other kind of support? In your heart, you will inevitably share what you have with your family, but at what cost to your health? Of course, you should if you can, but you should set parameters for your sanity as to how much of yourself you can give. Jesus gave until he could give no more. I am not sure your threshold of giving is at his level. However, you need to understand that giving so much of yourself may negatively impact you mentally and physically.

Think about the cost of your mental well-being. One-sided relationships are comprised of people who come to you at any time when they are in need. However, you can never go to them for any type of support. This is a relationship that is not healthy for you at all.

Relationships like these can drain you immensely and cause unnecessary pressure or stress in your life, creating unwarranted sadness or frustration. Many times, people lash out at their family or friends when these feelings of pressure boil over. You must examine these relationships closely so that you are not putting a strain on your health. You may be overextending yourself and draining your spirit. Do not get me wrong; please help all those you can help. But be aware of your limits. Know when you need to rest and when a relationship is no longer healthy for you to continue engaging in it without discovering how you are being impacted. Strive for your most intimate relationships to be created equal.

RELATIONSHIPS WITH YOUR ENEMY

God wants you to not only love and develop relationships with the people you know, but he also wants you to establish relationships with everyone, including those people who hate on you. Luke 6:35 states, "Love your enemies, and do good, and lend, expecting nothing in return, and your reward will be great, and you will be sons of the Most High, for he is kind to the ungrateful and the evil." God is asking us to love our enemies and give ourselves without recourse or regret. We should at least extend this courtesy to our loved ones without regret or feeling badly about it. When a relationship becomes too heavy to bear, discuss the next steps with God. Trust him to lead your relationship.

God, unlike man, does not need a 50–50 relationship. God wants a relationship with us even if it is one-sided. He shares his blessings even if we do not give anything back to him in return. If you do not believe me, look around you. The clothes on your back, the food you eat, the air you breathe—all belong to God and are provided because of his relationship with you, not specifically because of your relationship with him. Consider the parable of the prodigal son as an example of someone who was blessed even though he did not seemingly deserve it. God wants us to follow him now. However, he is there for us whenever we are ready to accept him; but do not let it be too late. Our goal of building relationships should be to imitate this type of heavenly relationship, where we can give to one another without expecting something in return. We should be there for one another with open arms, with the gift of forgiveness.

RELATIONSHIP WITH YOUR CHILD

Having a relationship with your children can also take a toll on you. Ask any parent, and they will tell you that parenting is not an easy task. It is probably the most rewarding and most frustrating job you will ever have. From the moment a child is conceived, you are no longer in charge of the relationship. You are excited to see the child, hold the child, feed the child, and watch it grow into the amazing being it will undoubtedly become (at least, that is your hope). However, a lot happens between the time a child is born and the exact time when the child leaves your home that can cause a great deal of grief.

The relationship with your child is just like a relationship with any other person. It needs to be managed and understood. However, the biggest difference is that you are playing a major role in the upbringing and survival of that child. The rearing of that child weighs heavily on how involved you are in that child's life. Many times, the parent-child relationship can become difficult, and parents need an outlet to better manage the relationship. This outlet can be a grandparent or other forms of help, like other similarly situated parents. Without that support system, managing the parent-child relationship can become worn and strenuous.

Understanding the dynamics of the relationship can be the difference between life and death. Unfortunately, many parents do not have an outlet or do not grasp the full undertaking of the parent-child relationship, especially when it comes to raising children. Without a support system, some parents tend to cause harm to themselves or the children.

The importance of this relationship may be explained in an article by Marisol Bello and Meghan Hoyer that examines more than three decades of FBI homicide data that show that on average, "four hundred fifty children are killed every year by their parents."[10] There are other compounding factors that play a role in these murders, like being addicted to drugs or having mental breakdowns. However, if the parents better understood the relationship with their children or reached out for a support system to guide them, the relationship with their children might improve. Providing an outlet to help the parents deal with whatever frustrations they are facing can potentially be the difference between saving lives and losing lives. Striving for happiness and understanding in these relationships is crucial for so many of the challenges with which we are dealing in this country.

PARENTING IN SWITZERLAND

Parents' relationships with their children are different across ethnicities, cultures, socioeconomic statuses, and geographies. When my wife and I traveled to Switzerland, we paid attention to the parental relationships there. The Swiss and American cultures are completely different. Switzerland appeared to be a laid-back country in many respects. The Swiss seemed not to worry about much, dissimilar to the way Americans stress about many things in life.

10. Bello and Hoyer, "Parents Who Do the Unthinkable."

One evening, my wife and I were at a restaurant, and we paid particular attention to a family sitting across from us. We were new parents at the time, and the Swiss family was eating with their daughter, who was similar in age to our daughter. The young Swiss girl would continuously leave the table where her parents were eating and would go out of the restaurant to ride her scooter. She rode the scooter in the restaurant as well. The waitress and restaurant manager could have cared less about the young girl riding around. My wife and I talked about how different that relationship was from the one we have.

We were raised in a stringent family, with rules that do not bend—especially when you are in front of other people or company. Our daughter would not dare ride her scooter in the restaurant, and we would not be comfortable with her riding it outside while we were sitting in the restaurant having dinner.

Our child-rearing practices were quite different than those of the Swiss family. It is not to say one way is better than the other. It is to say that we have different relationships with our children, and every set of parents must understand the dynamics of the relationship with their own children in order to have the best outcome.

MY CHILDREN

My children are the loves of my life, the apples of my eye, and all the other adorable sayings you can say to describe affectionate feelings toward your children. However, there are times when they can frustrate me. The children scream at each other, fight over toys, and roughhouse without regard to anything in the house, especially their health. This type of behavior being displayed by children is a lot for any parent to deal with after a particularly long day at work. However, children do not care about your long day at work—and, at this young age, they should not. They care only about living in the moment of today. As the younger child ages, she becomes bolder and challenges her older sister in everything. However, before she gets in trouble for anything she has done, she tells you that she loves you with the most affectionate hug you can imagine. This is the innocence and manipulation of a child.

In the midst of that roughhousing, unruliness, and destruction, parents must remember that these are just kids. We cannot look at children as if they are adults. They may be completely unaware of the consequences of their actions as well. If discipline needs to occur, Proverbs 29:15 states, "The rod and reproof give wisdom, but a child left to himself brings shame to his mother."

As parents, we should discipline our children, and they should obey us. When either the discipline or the reproof is lacking, you are raising a child that may one day bring shame to your family. As Colossians 3:20 explains, "Children, obey your parents in everything, for this pleases the Lord." My wife always says, "God makes these children look just like you so that no matter how upset you are, you can't do too much to them." She also stated when the five-year-old was just a few weeks old that she "couldn't wait to hear our daughter's voice." Five years later, we were both seeking ways to stop her from talking so much. This is a clear example of being careful for what you ask.

My girls are bright children. It is remarkable to see that your children seem to be learning at a much faster pace than you did when you were their ages. They also tend to take the knowledge they have acquired and use it against you as often as they can. There are many pleasures in being a parent, but there are many difficulties as well. There will be preteen, teenage, and young adult years that will affect your relationship in so many ways. The best advice here is to be the best parents you can be and develop a system or network of other parents, family, or friends that you can lean on for support. Do not allow a moment of disappointment or unhappiness with your children ruin your relationship forever.

INFUSE GOD IN YOUR PARENTING RELATIONSHIP

Trust in God and have an open dialogue with him about your feelings and your relationship with your children. Perhaps having someone who can provide you with some adult companionship may also help. You will need an outlet when parenting. It takes some time to figure it out, but the children are learning just as you are. They do not have a book on parents or how far they should take things before they are reprimanded. Their natural curiosity and rebelliousness will often clash with your rules. Learning how to deal with these instances with patience, love, and understanding is key to parenting.

The parent-child relationship will challenge your happiness every day. But the more you know about the relationship, the better. Parents must be slow to anger, even if that is the first emotion that shows itself. We must have the ability to walk away and regroup. There are too many stories of parents harming or killing their children because the child would not stop crying or did not follow the rules. A child is just that, a child. God does not kill us every time we fail to live up to his expectations. He forgives us repeatedly. Even when we are wrong, he gives us his love. We must adopt this behavior when we are dealing with our children, even during difficult times. The joys of parenting will help you overcome any hardships you may face along the way. When you factor in the context of nature vs. nurture, the lasting principle of being a parent comes from Proverbs 22:6, which states, "Train a child in the way he should go; even when he is old he will not depart from it."

PATERNAL RELATIONSHIP

Another key relationship that is often broken and is taking a toll on society is the relationship between a father and his child. This relationship is vital to the well-being of children, and I believe it is critical to the destiny of mankind. Yet so many men take this relationship and the responsibility of being a parent for granted. The devastating effects of an absent father weigh heavily on the livelihoods of mothers, sons, and daughters.

Young boys often tend to grow up resenting their fathers. Once the respect is lost, sometimes it is lost for good. The son may end up following a similar parental pattern as the one his father established and become an absent father as well. All the while, the son will never fully realize the importance of his presence in his own children's lives.

Daughters are also severally impacted by the absence of a good father figure. Young girls may end up seeking fatherly love or an unhealthy bond from other men because their fathers were not there to show them what love is or what love is supposed to be. It is said that many women who struggle in relationships with men as an adult attribute their broken relationship with their father as a contributing factor to their current situation. A father's role in his child's life is irreplaceable. Out of everything that is wrong with the current state of the world, it is the role of a loving father that can change it all, for better or for worst.

ARE YOU CREATING A SERIAL KILLER?

A father's relationship is so important to the upbringing of a child that you literally could be creating the difference between someone who can change the world for the better or someone who will eventually cause complete devastation. The understanding of just how important a role being a good father plays in the lives of their children can stem from recognizing the characteristics of a serial killer or mass murderer.

Most mass murderers are single or divorced. They do not have a relational support system in place.[11] It is not because they do not want a relationship. Human nature desires a relationship with another being. However, they are not able to establish or maintain a healthy relationship for one reason or another. Perhaps they grew up in an environment where relationships were broken. Jeffery Dahmer's parents were divorced, and Ted Bundy grew up in a single-parent household. These guys are infamous serial killers, and the lack of a strong and positive relationship may have played a role in their acts. If you show your child actions that simulate your marriage not having any meaning, then they may also grow up believing that marriage or a strong relationship means nothing. Therefore, they may not feel a need to develop a relationship with someone who may make them a better person.

The strength of a healthy marriage lends itself to keeping each significant other on the straight and narrow and picking each other up when the other is down. When times get hard, as they may, your significant other can be a shoulder to lean on. Many mass murderers do not have anyone to lean on for positive support or guidance.

However, they are typically extremely smart and have an extraordinarily high IQ. So you can either raise that child with the high IQ to change the world for the better or he or she will take that IQ and create chaos for the world to see.

Many mass murderers come from dysfunctional families with absent fathers or neglectful fathers. It for this very reason I urge fathers not to play the role of being absent within the lives of their children and always to remain a present force. If not, you could be leaving the rest of us with an uncontrollable maniac. Fathers should always seek a thriving existence in the child's life no matter if you and the child's mother cannot work it out. Some serial murders or mass murders have alcoholic fathers, and they are often loners. The overindulgence of alcohol tends to lead to a father becoming abusive, which may lead your child to adopt similar behaviors later in life.

I implore fathers to show their children the right way to engage in a relationship and create habits that enable them to grow into productive citizens by respecting and loving other people. No child is a loner if its father is around to be its parent and its friend.

JUST BE THERE

Fathers must understand that they are needed for more than just giving a little child support money here and there. Even if the father is present within

---

11. Eric, "Eleven Common Traits."

the home, he can still be emotionally removed from his family, either by working too much or just simply not being there enough. He tends to lose touch with how essential the simple act of being there for his family is. The lack of love and emotional availability can cause fathers to commit heinous acts without thinking about the damage they are doing. It is well known that, during domestic altercations, fathers are often personally responsible for harming their own families.

The previously mentioned *USA Today* study that explained how parents kill over 450 of their children annually also stated that fathers are the main culprits behind these killings. Men killed six out of ten children, most often beating or shooting them. Fathers or father-figures were at fault in 75 percent of cases when children were shot to death by a parent and in 64 percent of cases when a child was beaten.[12] Jay-Z says in his song "Meet the Parents," "Be a father you are killing your sons."[13] No truer words have been spoken, as fathers are directly killing their children. The father-child relationship can be linked to the bond that keeps society together. According to Jack Levin, a Northeastern University criminologist, "Violence is a masculine pursuit."[14] If a father establishes a relationship with his children, it becomes much more difficult to kill the children. If you as a father are present in the children's lives and have effectively established a bond, you should realize that the parent-child relationship is one where you are needed to be the leader and the giver of love.

Fathers must understand how much of a valuable component of their children's lives they are. They must accept the fact that nothing can replace them within the structure of a family. Some fathers become possessive and begin to develop other kinds of destructive thoughts like, "If I can't love you, no one else will." This phrase is often said to the mother, but the children are usually the ones who pay for this threat. This thought process is not an indication of love. This thought process is hate trying to wear love's garments.

There is truth to the concept of "if you love someone, they will come back." There is no need to kill someone you are supposed to love because they are leaving you for one reason or another. Life does not begin, nor should it end, in that moment of relational disagreement. The purpose of your relationship is meant to be more than that moment. However, life is too often cut short due to one person saying she or he is going to leave the other. Interpersonal rejection is a driving force behind so many murders across this country. Men, we have to do better.

12. Bello and Hoyer, "Parents Who Do the Unthinkable."
13. Carter and Smith, "Meet the Parents."
14. Bello and Hoyer, "Parents Who Do the Unthinkable."

FATHERLESS EPIDEMIC

To illustrate how dismal the situation is regarding America's families having stable households in which children and families can thrive, Gretchen Livingston, a senior researcher at Pew Research Center, states, "Fewer than half (46 percent) of U.S. kids younger than eighteen years of age are living in a home with two married heterosexual parents in their first marriage. This is a marked change from 1960 when 73 percent of children fit this description, and 1980, when 61 percent did."[15] She also found that one of the largest shifts in family structure is related to unmarried parents. Thirty-four percent of children today are living with an unmarried parent—up from just 9 percent in 1960, and 19 percent in 1980. You can see the trend here.

In most cases, the unmarried parents are single and have found another person. Perhaps this other love is a saving grace. But what happened to the structure of the family? What happened to the relationships here? Why is the family broken and the country is left to suffer from this lack of relational ties between a mother and father or between a husband and wife, thus impacting the relationship between a father and his child? Many people go through life believing their actions have nothing to do with society.

This is a gross misrepresentation of the facts. We are ultimately tied together through relationships, whether we know each other or not. For example, Adam Lanza, son of Peter and Nancy Lanza, is now known as the Sandy Hook mass murderer. Adam, who was a twenty-year-old young man, incomprehensively murdered twenty-six people, including many young children, at Sandy Hook Elementary on December 12, 2014. Scott Stump, a writer for NBC Universal, wrote an article mentioning the length of time Peter spent away from son. Stump wrote that Peter Lanza "had not seen his son in two years prior to this heinous act."[16] Two years is a long time to go without seeing your son or having any interaction in his life. I do not intend to judge Peter Lanza. This is also not to say there is a direct correlation or to insinuate he could have stopped Adam from committing such an atrocity. However, a father's influence and his relationship with his children are unlike any other. Perhaps being able to turn to his father would have been helpful, although we will never know. What I am certain of is that a father's presence can make all the difference in a child's life.

Single Mother Guide finds, "The single parent lifestyle which was once largely limited to poor women and minorities is now becoming the new

---

15. Livingston, "Fewer than Half."
16. Stump, "I Wish He Had."

norm."[17] The following statistics are mind-blowing in terms of showing how living in a fatherless home not only plagues children, it also significantly impacts the well-being of a family and the overall economy. Single Mother Guide finds the following:

- About four out of ten children are born to unwed mothers. Nearly two-thirds are born to mothers under the age of thirty.
- Of all single-parent families in the US, single mothers make up the majority.
- According to the US Census Bureau, out of about twelve million single-parent families in 2014, more than 80 percent were headed by single mothers.
- Today, one in four children under the age of eighteen—a total of about 17.4 million—are being raised without a father and nearly half (45 percent) live below the poverty line.

The consequences of this relationship are so vital to the progression of humanity, yet a growing number of men miss the mark.

WITHOUT MY FATHER

Speaking firsthand as someone who was raised in a fatherless home, the mounting frustration can sometimes get the best of you. I found myself looking for someone to call father or looking for a male role model throughout my childhood. In my mom's search for love and trying to find someone with whom to build a family, I can recall asking her whether I could call my one-year-old sister's father *my* father. I was about eleven at the time and was still searching for a father figure.

That conversation was a humbling experience for her. Suffice it to say, the relationship with my sister's father did not work out. Without a father there for whom I could develop an appreciation, I began to appreciate my mom even more for all she did for me. People would say to me that she is your mother and your father, and I would accept that description of her role in my life, because she was making sure that all my essential needs were met.

But now I am a father, and I better understand the necessity of a father's role in his child's life. I have a complete appreciation for how valuable a father is to his children. A father's presence is not only welcomed by the child but by the mother as well. Raising a kid on your own is a very daunting task for anyone.

17. SingleMotherGuide, "Single Mother Statistics."

I would never discredit my mother or the work she did in caring for me; however, a father provides a sense of balance for his child. This balance is critical for a child's upbringing. Knowing your father cares and loves you provides a child with the support system needed to overcome many of life's obstacles.

SEARCHING FOR A FATHER

Sometimes children look for a father figure in several places. They turn to their friends, older siblings, a friend's father, their pastor, or some other male figure as a source to fill this void. These relationships can be healthy and productive. Unfortunately, we have also heard of stories where these relationships are unhealthy. Often, children will seek acceptance and love in gangs and other social constructs when a father is not present. Children will always seek that emotional connection to a strong father figure or someone to whom they can look up. I was no different.

My mother raised me, and I have plenty of uncles, but the first man to ask me about my grades or my performance in school was my high school football coach, Reverend William Wrighten (he was not a reverend at the time). I never knew how powerful the presence of a positive caring male figure could be for a young man before my coach asked what seemed like a nonchalant question. I never told him how life-changing his simple inquiry was to me. I was always a good student, but having him show a little thought or care about how I was performing in school was unfamiliar to me. I still think about it to this day and would like to thank Coach Wrighten for showing a young kid from Blakely—the neighborhood of my youth—that men do care about the children in their community. Since then, I have had other men step up and show different forms of fatherly support or male guidance.

In this regard, I consider myself lucky, because I know there are a lot of young men who do not have anyone to whom to turn for help and must figure out life on their own or through the lens of someone who does not have their best interests in mind. Even as a professional and throughout my career, I have had great mentors show me different ways to live and be a better man, either by example or through interactions with their own family.

Today, I have a relationship with my father. It is a relationship that is still being cultivated, but better late than never. The time it takes for a child to heal from the wounds of being fatherless will probably last forever.

A FATHER'S DAY MESSAGE

On Father's Day in 2016, my cousin-in-law sent a group text message that speaks volumes about the role God plays in our lives when it comes to developing a relationship with your father. His text was copied from *Honest to God?: Becoming an Authentic Christian*, written by Pastor Bill Hybels, which states the following:

> To a generation of men failed by their fathers and lost in a cloud of confusion, God says, "Don't spend a lifetime in aimless drifting. Don't succumb to mindless misinterpretations of masculine identity. Enter into a relationship with me, through Jesus Christ, and allow me to lead you into authentic manhood. Become my adopted sons and let me 're-father' you."[18]

I chose a similar path to the one mentioned in the text. The concept of God re-fathering you is an interesting one that speaks to the depth of developing a relationship with God. I needed God to lead me through some difficult trials while being without a father and facing life as the man of the house. Even though I considered myself the man of the house, I did not completely understand my role.

I would like to think that I grew up when my grandmother died in 1995. I was twelve at the time and had to start thinking about my life as a man. I would ask myself what I needed to do to help my mother survive while raising our family. I would pray or write my thoughts out on paper in what would later become my first—hopefully not my last—poetry book. The "Conversations with God" section was the shortest portion of my book. I guess it represented where I was in my journey with God at the time. However, my conversations with God were enough to strengthen and help me overcome my tribulations without my father. They even strengthened me at times when I felt like there was nowhere else for me to turn when life was difficult. Proverbs 4:1–5 states:

> Hear, O sons, a father's instruction, and be attentive, that you may gain insight, for I give you good precepts; do not forsake my teaching. When I was a son with my father, tender, the only one in the sight of my mother, he taught me and said to me, "Let your heart hold fast my words; keep my commandments, and live. Get wisdom; get insight; do not forget, and do not turn away from the words of my mouth."

---

18. Hybels, *Honest to God*.

These verses spoke to me as I considered God to be my Father in heaven and on earth. Where else was I to turn? There was not someone in the flesh to whom I could go for fatherly support. I came to rely on my relationship with God for support and stability. I needed to find that guided support from God, whom I have since called my true Father.

Men often fail to understand the value of the relationship between a father and child—God does not fail to understand it—and America can no longer afford for this to be the case.

RELATIONSHIP WITH MANKIND

Relationships with mankind are especially important as the Bible discusses fellowship and bringing others to Christ as the ultimate mission of a Christian. However, developing a relationship with God is of the utmost importance. It will help you deal with any relationship you have here on earth, whether as parent and child or husband and wife. God will prepare you for everything that you will face in this life and align that with his ultimate purpose for you in the next life.

Fathers, take heed and love your children. Love your wife as God loves the church, and create a happy household for your entire family, which will be supported by a strong relationship with God. The impact of your relationship with your family may save thousands of lives and may even change the world.

RACE: AMERICA'S FALTERED RELATIONSHIP

Historically, America has had relationship problems within its borders. As great a country as America touts itself to be, it has always failed at developing relationships among its citizens. There has always been a system of societal prejudice, there has always been a class system, and there has always been a racial divide. The very notion of this country's existence is based on race, and the fact that people are classified by their race shows how much of an ineffectual design this country has developed. Whether everyone agrees or not, America was founded by people who used and abused people of another race. It was also stolen from its native people. If your country's roots and its foundation are grounded in hate, how do you find love among people who have been inciting and suffering from hate since the beginning?

America did not invent slavery, but it was used to build this country. Slavery was used as an American financial crux or source of economic enhancement for the wealthy. It was also a tool that perpetuated hate and segregation. Slavery, in its chain and shackle definition, is no longer part of America's culture, but the hate and subsequent inequality derived from slavery have never left this country. Our race relations have always been troubling despite the progress that has been made through decades of civil rights battles and countless sacrifices.

America's culture feeds on pitting one race against another, and it seems to be at a precipice. But this behavior is not new. Racial relations were much worse for our ancestors in this country. However, the events of today are more egregious, because we should be progressing as a nation. But as the saying goes, if you do not learn from history, you are doomed to repeat it.

I believe we are repeating history over and over because we refuse to learn from it. I once heard acclaimed actor Morgan Freeman state in an interview with late-night television host Stephen Colbert, "America is going through with this level of hate, and political turmoil is nothing to be alarmed by. This country has always been one of ebbs and flows." Well, if he is correct regarding his assessment, America is within a deep ebb. This country consistently gives both the power to hate and hateful ideologies like racism.

RACISM IS AN IDEOLOGY, CONTRIBUTING TO OUR UNHAPPINESS

Americans act as if racism is a real thing. Racism is not real. It is a made-up idea that misinformed parents teach their children and then pass on for generations. It is a fictitious conceptualization being perpetrated and demonstrated by people who refuse to progress and accept that being from a certain race, creed, or color does not dictate who you are as a person. I liken racism to the idea of Santa Claus—not Saint Nicholas, who was an actual person, but the classic portrayal of Santa Claus. As children, you believe in Santa because your parents tell you there is a jolly guy in a red suit who delivers presents for Christmas. Racism is taught with a dogmatic conviction similar to the idea of Santa. It does not exist without someone breathing life into the idea.

Children are not born knowing they are of a different race from other children. As I stated, my children have friends of every shade, race, and ethnicity. The only thing they know about the other children that separate one child from another is their names. At this point, they do not even believe in the idea of there being boy toys or activities versus girl toys or activities. Of course, this understanding will change with the boxed thinking of societal gender normality. My children have never once said this child was

Caucasian or White, African, Asian, Indian, Hispanic, or some other ethnicity of American. They can see that people come in different colors, but they do not associate their friends' skin colors with their character.

The separation of ethnicities, thus infusing racism, does not exist without parents and a racial society determined to bring about a racial divide. Just like Santa does not exist without parents, racism does not exist without someone pushing the idea. For example, the two guys that shot and killed Ahmaud Arbery were father and son. The son was of an age where he could have decided to not harm Ahmaud, but he was taught by his father that black people were less than they were, thus bringing about a generational relationship with racist beliefs. It takes dedication and a purposeful stoking of the fire to keep the idea of racism alive. A significant difference between these two fictional ideas of Santa and racism is that Santa should represent hope and happiness to children around the world, and racism brings hate and poverty. Both are fictional ideologies upon which we continuously build. The sad thing is that people stop believing in Santa at age six or seven, or if a child happens to catch its parents in the act of hiding gifts at an earlier age. However, racism is believed in and acted upon by adults. Think of how ridiculous an adult would look hoping for Santa to bring some presents for Christmas. This is exactly how foolish people look when racism is allowed to fester and have a place in our lives as adults.

On the other hand, hate is real. It is an innate feeling that we have and with which we are born. Hate is as simple as a child telling you that he does not like pureed green beans from Gerber at a young age. To hate or dislike something is a natural part of us, without being taught by anyone to have this feeling. The hate a child has for something he does not like is biological. However, hate becomes dangerous when it manifests itself within an imaginary concept like racism.

According to the Department of Justice Bureau of Justice Statistics, more than 250,000 Americans over the age of twelve are victimized every year by hate crimes.[19] This stat speaks to how integral the issue of hate is within our society. Children and young teenagers are dealing with this amount of vitriol in their lives. In 2015, according to the Southern Poverty Law Center, America had over 890 known hate groups in existence.[20] Not only is there hate, but we take the concept of hate and form groups of like-minded people who wish to do nothing more than hate other people. When we teach our children to hate other people, we are teaching them something about relationships that is not of God and could not be further from what

---

19. Sandholtz et al., "Hate Crime Victimization."
20. Southern Poverty Law Center, "Active Hate Groups."

is biblical—which is love. When hate is fed nonsensical ideas like racism, separation, and having classifications based on the have and have-nots, it creates a powerful mixture of pain.

Our relationship with each other is so intertwined that we must remove hate as a unified people to move forward as a nation. The people who stir up this ideology of racism and division are completely taking advantage of the disadvantaged. Be it financially, educationally, emotionally, or just through lack of access, these individuals who are suffering the most are also the ones who are most at risk.

The unfounded thoughts that lead to abuse and misuse pit one against another while fostering hate due to skin color, religion, sexual preference, or some other pointless classification and cannot be tolerated. We cannot continue to allow this form of made-up hate to be a part of our society, or we will forever be doomed to have strained racial relationships.

We will continue to kill one another in the name of superficial differences based on a made-up concept. For this country to reach its full potential and for the people of this country to be more like God, we must work on our racial relationships.

OUR RELATIONSHIP WITH GUNS

In addition to relationships of race, we must understand and fix relationships of all kinds. Americans have an unfathomable and unprecedented desire to kill one another. Gun violence in this country is by far the worst it has ever been. This country loves to express hate toward would-be terrorists but is not ready to stand up and face the truth of the terror plaguing this country from within its borders. Journalist Jennifer Mascia from the Trace (an organization after my own heart that focuses on gun-related news) wrote an article stating, "A total of 12,942 people have been killed in the United States in 2015 by gun homicide, unintentional shooting or murder/suicide."[21] Almost 13,000 people died from senseless acts of violence, and, many times, it was because of a broken relationship of some sort. It is tragic that on an average day in 2015, thirty-six Americas were killed by guns.

When you factor in the 20,000 people who ended their own lives, the amount of gun violence in this country is abhorrent. These people may have found another way to complete suicide if they did not have access to a gun. However, it is the accessibility to guns that compels the argument. Concerning the number of people who have died due to terrorist attacks, the

---

21. Mascia, "Fifteen Statistics."

Trace reports statistics measuring from 2005 to 2015 showing that only 71 Americans were killed in terrorist attacks on US soil.[22]

During that same period, 301,797 Americans were killed by gun violence.[23] According to a reference from PBS NewsHour that plotted the locations of mass shootings using data from a Mass Shooting Tracker data, there were 372 mass shootings in the US in 2015, killing 475 and wounding 1,870.[24] The year 2015 was a terrible year for America, and we seem to be getting worse as a country. America's relationship with guns is intolerable, but we hide this intolerance behind the Second Amendment.

However, when the Second Amendment was written, the forefathers of this country had no idea what would transpire with the advancement of our weaponry. The number of deaths on American soil committed by Americans should make us ask who the real terrorists are and whom we should consider as the most significant threat to American lives. These numbers tell a clear story of from where the actual terror is coming, and it is within our walls.

SHOOTINGS BY POLICE

With the prevalence of social media, police officers have been under the microscope due to the rising number of unarmed deaths in this country. Somashekhar and Rich, journalists for the *Washington Post*, captured the essence of this growing issue in an article stating that "more than 250 people were fatally shot by police during the first three months of 2016."[25] If the killings continue at that pace, over 1,000 people will be shot and killed by law enforcement by the end of the year. This is a rate of eighty-three people per month dying at the hands of those that serve and protect. The *Post* article also states, "In 2015, 986 people were killed by police."[26] The clear majority were armed and half of them were white, but the other half leaves us with more questions than answers.

This relationship problem is so bleak that our country is viewed by other global citizens as an unsafe place to live. In addition to the armed white people who were killed, nearly 40 percent of the black men who were killed by police were unarmed.[27] Forty percent of unarmed deaths is an in-

22. Mascia, "Fifteen Statistics."
23. Mascia, "Fifteen Statistics."
24. Oldham, "Two Thousand Fifteen."
25. Somashekhar and Rich, "Final Tally."
26. Somashekhar and Rich, "Final Tally."
27. Somashekhar and Rich, "Final Tally."

credible number. America has been ravaged lately with stories and accounts of deadly police encounters by all races, but people of color are disproportionately suffering under these circumstances.

We desperately need to work on repairing the strained relationship of the police and the citizens they serve to move forward as a country. We are not in opposition to each other. There are officers who practice racist ideologies and have predetermined prejudice notions that breed hate and contribute to unnecessary killings. However, there are good officers and good people of color. There are black law enforcement officers as well. Law enforcement and people of color should not be natural-born enemies. It is not innate to hate or harm one another. These are behaviors that are being promoted and acted upon by people who do not have the best intentions for the future of this country. These hateful acts are being incensed by people who want to stop the progression of a unified America, under God, indivisible, as the Pledge of Allegiance says. They would rather risk an upheaval that could be devastatingly catastrophic for America. The land of the free is truly captivated by the liberty of killing one another, when it should be focused on uplifting each other.

INTIMATE MURDERS

Our children and our women are at elevated risk as well. At a rate of more than twice a day, someone under eighteen is shot and killed, according to Mike Brunker, a reporter from NBC News.[28] We have to find a remedy to this issue with numbers like these staring us in the face. Our elected officials have talked about gun violence, but the country has seen little action in trying to stymie these occurrences other than rhetoric. However, I believe eliminating gun violence must remain a priority for the American government. Our children are dying at an incomprehensible pace. According to NBC News journalists DeFrank and Brunker, "Seventy-five percent of children killed with guns in 2015 were under age twelve."[29] These children did not reach their teenage years before their lives were taken away from them. Gun Violence Archive references that at least 756 American children were killed by gunfire in 2015.[30] Think about that devastation.

The women of this country are at risk of elevated violence as well. Journalist Erika Eichelberger wrote an article called "Violence on the Home Front," where she indicates that between 2005 and 2010, "Sixty

28. DeFrank and Brunker, "Since Sandy Hook."
29. DeFrank and Brunker, "Since Sandy Hook."
30. Gun Violence Archive, "About."

percent of all violent injuries in this country were inflicted by loved ones or acquaintances."[31] Nothing speaks more highly of an existing relationship problem than the fact that loved ones commit violence against each other at such a high rate. The article explained that, in 2011, 79 percent of murders reported to the FBI (in which the victim-offender relationship was known) were committed by friends, loved ones, or acquaintances. To home in on the point of violence toward women, Eichelberger adds, "Sixty-four percent of the women killed every year are murdered by family members or lovers." How could our relationships erode so much that the giver of life is one of the main targets of violence? The strain of a man's relationship with women must change. God has asked us to cherish our mothers and honor our wives. Do you love your mother, do you honor your wife? I believe we have failed to keep up our end of the bargain.

How are men able to kill their families with complete disregard to the love they are supposed to provide? Life will never present us with a situation where our only recourse is to kill our families. When a man resorts to this type of behavior, these actions are driven solely by his desires. There are more than 1,000 homicides of that kind annually, or 2.73 murders of women committed each day. Every day, a mother, daughter, or wife is being slaughtered at the hands of someone with whom she has a personal relationship.

Eichelberger also points out that if there is a gun in a home where domestic abuse is a common thing, a woman is eight times more likely to be killed. America has created a haven filled with violence toward women. How far have we strayed from the mandate of God regarding loving our wives? Colossians 3:19 says "Husbands, love your wives, and do not be harsh with them." This is a direct biblical requirement and one that many men fail to uphold.

Men, please take heed to these stats of how many women are killed at the hands of their loved ones. Please love your women: stop killing them. America—or any country, for that matter—should not be able to stand for this type of behavior. The Bible teaches "thou shalt not kill" as a component of the Ten Commandments. It is incredible how we forget the basic principles of biblical life, especially when it comes to our women and the basic idea of not killing. Stronger relationships with one another can help us become better people, inspiring each of us to find what we are looking for within ourselves. These broken relationships lead to unhappiness in so many forms. We must remain steadfast in building fruitful relationships in this world, especially when it comes to our women.

---

31. Eichelberger, "Violence on Home Front."

SOCIOECONOMIC STATUS

There are other societal issues that contribute to being in a state of unhappiness. Many people allow possessions to dictate their happiness. The 1974 song "Be Thankful for What You Got," written by William DeVaughn, speaks volumes about our emotional ties to having things. We are constantly seeking ways to acquire more things. But if we were to look at life in terms of where people live geographically, we would see that the desire to acquire more things and the types of things we acquire would be drastically different.

For example, if you live in a big house with a picket fence, what you value or consider a materialistic purchase may be a little different than someone who lives in an impoverished neighborhood. However, people who live behind a picket fence also have issues, just like other people who may not have as many possessions. Famed comedian Kevin Hart lived in a secluded residential area with security guards. Over the same weekend of the release of his movie *Central Intelligence*, someone broke into his home and stole over $500,000 worth of personal items.

Kevin Hart may have been upset over someone burglarizing his home because his sense of security was completely compromised. However, later that same week, Kevin Hart was on the *Steve Harvey Morning Show* being his charismatic self. Perhaps he did not attach himself to the material things that were taken from him? Perhaps he thought he could later replace those objects? Or maybe it was a combination of both. But the one thing I noticed about him was the calmness in his personality. He remained the same jovial person the world knows Kevin Hart to be. He did not let this incident get the best of him.

He could have chosen to be unhappy about his unfortunate circumstances. But instead of being unhappy, he chose to press on. He later mentioned in another interview, "Those stolen items were just stuff." He can get those things back. They do not mean anything in the grand scheme of life. This is the mentality I desire everyone to possess. The message here is that we cannot be defeated by unhappiness when something unfortunate happens with our stuff. After all, it is just stuff. God has something more in store for us than the stuff to which we are tied. Someone can steal your material possessions, but no one can take what God has ordained to be yours.

It is easy to be unhappy when crimes are occurring in your neighborhood and people are killing each other every day. I completely understand the turmoil this living situation can have on your psyche. The people who are committing these crimes are unhappy with their surroundings as well. Their unhappiness is part of the reason they are committing these crimes against you and their community. They do not understand or appreciate that we are in this world together as social beings tied to each other. Their lack of appreciation for you as a brother or sister leads to unsavory behaviors. This reasoning does not validate or excuse their actions; however, they have developed a mindset of carelessness due in part to their socioeconomic status.

Instead of retaliating or creating a place of unhappiness, we can all take the same route as Kevin Hart in terms of how we view material things. Sure, Kevin Hart may have more money than most people, but look beyond the idea of money. His heart was in the right place when factoring in overcoming an unfortunate incident. We cannot allow our present circumstances to dictate our future. You should be able to trust in God and believe in his purpose, so that your happiness is not tied to where you live or what you have.

FINDING HAPPINESS NO MATTER WHERE YOU LIVE

Your socioeconomic status should not control your emotional well-being. Nor should you shroud yourself in a state of unhappiness or depression due to your socioeconomic state. You will not be able to see a better way out if you are constantly bombarding your thoughts with the idea of being defeated. I grew up in Williamsburg County, which was the poorest county in South Carolina. And South Carolina also happened to be the forty-second poorest state in the US.

There are some people with whom I grew up who went on to do well in life, and there were others who did not make the best decisions with their lives. My hometown in Williamsburg County usually stacks the chips against you when you are trying to succeed in life, through a lack of resources, encouragement, or circumstances. The disadvantages of living there could be felt and seen far and wide. When your life is faced with seemingly insurmountable economic obstacles, it is valuable to have a support system. It is truly a blessing when you have people who care about you, a supportive family, or healthy relationships with friends that can help you get through the tough times when you are raised in a lower socioeconomic class. These relationships with my support system helped me to resist the influence of poverty and all that it brings. I was able to forge another path and resisted becoming a child of an impoverished statistic.

To this day, my upbringing continues to push me. However, I now live in one of the richest states in the US and one of the wealthiest counties within the state. Talk about a reversal of fortune just based on where you live!

I cannot say I changed my circumstances on my own. My wife has been incredible every step of the way in my life. This is a relationship that has allowed me time to grow and strengthen myself as a person. At one point in my life, when I was not feeling optimistic about my circumstances, my wife said, "I was taken from you [like Eve, taken from the side of Adam], so it is my job to restore you. If I am not restoring you, then I would be cancer to you, and what good is that."

That statement signifies her true love and support, and I thank her for always being there. But more than my wife's contributions to our family's life, God has not wavered either. And because of his support, I am determined to not allow circumstances to dictate happiness.

Build upon your relationships and move beyond your socioeconomic status as being a hindrance for you to achieve what God has for you. Even if you do not have a supportive significant other currently, I urge you to try God. His love is so much more than ours and makes up for whatever we may be missing from any other person. God desires to use those who have less than others and set them up to do great things in this world for his glory. Try God!

SEEK JOY, NOT HAPPINESS

Being in a constant state of unhappiness tends to lend itself to depression if not treated or examined by a mental health professional. I do not intend to diagnose depression, but I want you to understand that you control your happiness. It must be an internal decision that you make. Ultimately, you do not want to be satisfied with being happy; you want to find joy. For joy, unlike happiness, is more than a feeling; it is a part of you. When you have joy, people who see you out and about will know that joy runs through your veins. It will radiate from you, whether you are smiling or not.

Being unhappy will not be an option, since you know that joy comes in the morning and all things on this earth are temporary. As a kid in school, you may be influenced by the distractions of bullying or being mistreated; however, when you have joy, even the meanest of bullies cannot take away what makes you tick. Your most offensive or depressing setback is nothing more than a test for you to overcome it with joy. Knowing joy will comfort you when there is no one else around. It comes from God and is stored in your heart. When joy can occupy your thoughts, the world around you will become a better place.

Your relationships will begin to experience love like they never have before. You will develop more patience to deal with your children, friends, and other family members. Joy helps you see the good in others, no matter their race, creed, or color. Joy does not need a gun. Joy overcomes pain and socioeconomic distress. Joy will comfort you and allow you to show comfort to others, no matter how challenging the relationship may be. Joy wants to be a permanent placement within your life. However, it is not something that is obtained overnight. It is something that must be worked on as you continue to develop a relationship with God.

Again, joy comes from God, which is why no person or circumstance can take it from you. Only you can choose to not have joy; but why would you do such a thing? You can call on joy any time of the day and through every situation you face in your life. Even when faced with the death of a loved one or perhaps your own end-of-life situation, joy will support you. It will help you to understand that God did not allow these major life challenges to happen without cause. Whether we understand God's intent or not, joy is ever present.

JOY IN THE FACE OF DEVASTATION

On June 12, 2016, a terrorist committed a hate-filled act in Orlando at Club Pulse. A gunman killed forty-nine people in what was then deemed to be the worst mass shooting in US history. This incident will forever be marked in America's history. We may never know God's purpose for allowing such a travesty to happen. However, a step in the right direction is that the American Public Health Association has now deemed gun violence to be a public health crisis, and there is mounting pressure to remove assault weapons from the public. This is a huge step in dealing with gun violence in America. I do not know what the outcome will be, but, hopefully, we will not have any more tragedies of this kind. This little acknowledgment of the gun violence epidemic is the hope of a coming joy, when we do not have to deal with these issues.

James 1:2–3 states, "Cout it all joy, my brothers, when you meet trials of various kinds, for you know that the testing of you faith produces steadfastness. And let steadfastness have its full effect, that you may be perfect and complete, lacking in nothing." For an example of faith unwavering, remember the strength and mercy of the survivors and loved ones from the Charleston church shooting on June 17, 2015. During prayer service at Emanuel African Methodist Episcopal, a mass murderer filled with hate and believing in racism shot and killed nine people worshiping. During the trial, the daughter of one of the victims said they forgave the shooter. Forgiveness and mercy are components of joy. Without those two acts of kindness, joy cannot be attained. I cannot say my soul has reached that depth; however, those are the actions of someone who has attained God's true joy and understanding.

Seek joy from God and not happiness from people or earthly possessions; then watch how your life will be transformed. The key to not being in a state of unhappiness and allowing that empty emotion to dictate our livelihoods is to be filled with joy. Romans 15:13 says it best: "May the God of hope fill you with all joy and peace in believing, so that by the power of the Holy Spirit you may abound in hope." Joy brings about hope, and hope is the thing that will encourage you to change your circumstances and strengthen your relationships.

Pundits say the children of Chicago do not have hope, which is why they lash out against one another and their environment. We must allow joy to overcome the storm and instill hope within the streets of Chicago, Baltimore, and everywhere within the borders of this country. We are seeking happiness in the wrong places. Find joy and hold on to its unchanging hand—for joy, your joy, comes from God.

Challenge 3

Chasing Money

Money Never Fulfills You

What are your goals in life? So many of us say that we want to be a millionaire so often that a hit TV show was created asking that same question, *Who Wants to Be a Millionaire?* The lottery gives Vegas a run for its money when you consider how many people spend their hard-earned dollars hoping to make it big. The lottery is big business for the government—which says a lot about its merits—especially when you consider the government's double-dipping in revenue for the purchase of the ticket and the taxes they garner if you were to win. According to the North American Association of State and Provincial Lotteries, "Lotteries took in $70.1 billion in sales in 2014."[1]

Lotteries, like many other financially predatory markets advertise heavily in poorer markets, preying on populations of people with less. We have become so engrossed with the idea of chasing money that we spend more on the lottery than many other forms of entertainment.[2] This statistic shows that we place a high priority on the idea of being rich or chasing money. However, this exercise of chasing money is oftentimes an unfulfilling pursuit that leaves us exhausted and broke. First Timothy 6:17 states, "As for the rich in this present age, charge them not to be haughty, nor to set their hopes on the uncertainty of riches, but on God, who richly provides

1. Thompson, "Lotteries."
2. Thompson, "Lotteries."

us with everything to enjoy." The Bible directly addresses this issue for us, yet we find other sources of enjoyment by chasing something that will never fulfill us.

We run the same rat race to which I alluded earlier just to chase money. You have probably heard of people who have won the lottery or had huge winnings from gambling unfortunately ending up right back where they started. You may have also heard stories concerning athletes who have amassed huge sums of money only to end up losing most, if not all, their fortune.

There are so many reasons people lose their recently acquired wealth. They may have family coming from every crack and crevice asking for financial help or support. They may have purchased extravagant items to show the world how much money they have. Or they may simply be terrible at money management.

Even professional money managers or famed stockbrokers have had their fair share of chasing money for the big win, only to lose in the end. Bernie Madoff comes to mind when thinking of someone who chased money and ended up on the losing end of the race. Many other stockbrokers or financial advisors have either killed themselves or done other harmful things to their families in the pursuit of money. When the window to cash in closes, all is usually lost.

How many CFOs and accountants have gone to jail for embezzlement? How many drug dealers have died over money? In urban neighborhoods, the chase for money in relation to drug dealing and the murderous consequences are dire. How many companies have gone bankrupt by being greedy and taking more than they should? There was the too-big-to-fail catastrophe surrounding these billion-dollar organizations being greedy and chasing money, only to corrupt the entire US financial market, which required an unprecedented bailout from taxpayers. To put it another way, the same people from whom they were taking money, with reckless abandon, ended up saving their companies. "From July 9, 2002 to July 2007, the Department of Justice's (DOJ) President's Corporate Fraud Task Force arrested some sixty-three ex-CFOs,"[3] according to CFO.com. These were the financial experts who were supposed to understand the value of money. However, even some of the most educated financial gurus failed to realize that chasing money is usually a dead end.

In fact, in the July 18, 2007, announcement, the DOJ said it counted 214 chief executives, 23 corporate counsels or attorneys, and 128 vice presidents as having been convicted since July 2002, in addition to at least 53 CFOs. This list is incredulous when you think of the amount of money

3. Plourd, "Count 'Em: Sixty-Three CFOs."

being exchanged at the expense of the entire global economy. The ex-CFOs on the DOJ list were confirmed as having been convicted of "charges that included conspiracy; insider trading; money laundering; racketeering; embezzlement; accessory to fraud; and bank, mail, wire, and securities fraud."[4]

You would figure these companies would tire of chasing money without thinking about how it would impact the world. But when you are in pursuit of an infinite passion that has no real basis or end goal, trying to become satisfied with a set amount is an exceedingly difficult undertaking. This was one rat race in which no one benefited, and it was all done for the sake of more money.

Titus 3:14 states, "And let our people learn to devote themselves to good works, so as to help cases of urgent need, and not be unfruitful." We did not learn from our past mistakes as a country, since we are embarking upon similar actions in dealing with our fiscal responsibilities.

During the final days of the recession, some companies were bailed out by the government to save the US economy, and others crashed and burned. The good times never seem to last when you are allowing money to run the operation. We must manage money and not let money manage us, whether through personal accounting, a professional money manager, or a corporation. Whatever the reason, chasing money solely to have more money seems to be fruitless, since the monies tend to outrun us every time.

LIVING PAYCHECK TO PAYCHECK

"I am so sick and tired of living paycheck to paycheck." Do you know someone or have you said these exact words regarding a financial situation? You are not alone in these sentiments; America has a high number of people living paycheck to paycheck. Angela Johnson, a CNN Money author, reports, "In June 2013 roughly three-quarters of Americans were living paycheck-to-paycheck, with little to no emergency savings."[5]

The article points out that over 240 million people live "check to check" in America. Families are on the brink of financial disaster in the richest country in the world. Johnson also states that "fewer than one in four Americans have enough money in their savings account to cover at least six months of expenses, enough to help cushion the blow of a job loss, medical emergency or some other unexpected event, according to the survey of 1,000 adults." It appears that the wealthiest country in the world is filled with cash poor citizens.

    4. Plourd, "Count 'Em: Sixty-Three CFOs."
    5. A. Johnson, "Seventy-Six Percent of Americans."

So, with such an elevated amount of karoshi and chasing money, how are we still living paycheck to paycheck? Something does not seem right. Johnson reports, "Fifty percent of those surveyed have less than a three-month cushion and 27 percent had no savings at all." This is the pain that grips America more than anything else. You cannot get over the hill no matter how hard you work, and it seems like the money you are making is never enough. We are killing ourselves working paycheck to paycheck without any room to enjoy the fruits of our labor. We are measuring ourselves against a system that is not set up for us to win.

Our frivolous goals in life make it exceedingly difficult to amass the type of success we desire. Success at this point is not a million dollars. Based on how little money we have; success is just trying to have enough money to cover any emergencies that may arise. How can you afford to save for retirement when you are barely making it day by day?

MY LIFE LIVING PAYCHECK TO PAYCHECK

As I stated, I lived in a poor area when I was a child, and my family did not have much in terms of economic value, so I am familiar with the concept of living paycheck to paycheck. None of my immediate family members had the same job for ten, fifteen, or twenty years; therefore, thinking about retirement, pensions, or 401ks was never really an option when I was growing up. Most of the time, getting money the best way you knew how would suffice on a day by day basis. Family members would work on someone's farm, help the local pig farmer, or sometimes go up to New York to help my aunt and uncle with their fruit and vegetable business.

Even though my mom was a hard worker, managing a nine-to-five and shuffling piddling odd jobs, none of it helped her to get over our family's financial burden. She worked at McDonald's and Hardee's simultaneously trying to build up her income, yet we were still living paycheck to paycheck. She did not have a particular skill set that would enable her to obtain a high-paying position. Having only a high school education, in a poor county, with limited opportunities, does not offer you much of a chance to expand your horizon. She possessed an unbelievable work ethic. However, her resourcefulness was not enough to help her escape the realities of financial difficulty, even though she was determined to be a provider for her children. She also worked at a Tupperware plant in Hemingway, SC, for a while. She would always find other ways to make money, but the money she earned was never enough.

Living paycheck to paycheck or not having a paycheck at all may allow people time to conjure up other ways to earn money. In some cases, people are not able to see a better way to make a living, thus believing they must turn to a life of crime to make ends meet. They genuinely believe this is the best way for them to make money or eat, as they would say on the street. No matter the catalyst when you are living paycheck to paycheck, life is a little harder.

For us, it was no different. As a child, I could not see the stress or pressures of trying to provide for a family, but, as I matured, the evidence was clear and the struggle was real. I came to realize that my mother had loans here, debts there, layaways, IOUs, and insufficient funds aplenty. It can be quite a burden when one person is trying to take care of a family.

CHASING LOVE OVER CHASING MONEY

Being rich may not be all that it is portrayed to be. Rapper J. Cole writes in his song "Love Yourz," "Sometimes being broke was better."[6] His story is one of the many rags-to-riches stories within America. In the song, he speaks insightfully about the ups and downs of being broke and rich. He takes the listener through the vantage point of both lifestyles and concludes, "Sometimes being broke was better." The idea of living paycheck to paycheck seemed to appeal to him or was less stressful, because there were fewer responsibilities and less pressure placed upon him. The reason for the ups and downs is because we are not supposed to be chasing money at all. Cole mentions love is all you need. He has a point; love is all you need in the end. Love helps you to realize that there is more to life than money. Besides, why would you chase money, when God takes care of all your needs?

Matthew 6:26 states, "Look at the birds of the air: they neither sow nor reap nor gather into barns, and yet your heavenly Father feeds them. Are you not of more value than they?" Birds do not sow or reap, but God makes sure they are fed. Are you not more valuable than a bird? Of course, you are—so stop chasing money. You really cannot take it with you when your time is up here on earth.

When people are dying, many of them desire the love and affection of their family members. All the things you were chasing will not be anywhere on your mind when your time comes; therefore, you should chase the things that mean the most to you—and money does not even come close. The only thing worth chasing is love.

6. Cole, "Love Yourz."

Love is the ultimate provider beyond all. Love erases the desire to chase money. I am not talking about love in the way you would say "I love you" to someone else. It is rather the absolute love that God gives to restore, empower, feed, and keep us.

Let us say you are lucky enough to work at one location while you are running your race to chase money, and a homeless person is living nearby. You pass this homeless individual almost every day. The individual does not work nor has a place to live. After a year, you still come across the same homeless individual sitting or standing in the same area. It is stated that the human body can only live for approximately twenty-one days without food and approximately seven days without water. However, this homeless person continued to eat and live day by day. It may not be a desirable lifestyle, but he is still living every day, nonetheless. Just like the birds, which do not sow or reap, you will notice that God has made provisions either by you or someone else's supplication to help the homeless person continue to survive. I am not saying you should be homeless to understand God's true love, but you should understand God's love is always there, no matter your situation.

Therefore, chasing money is not a goal that you should set for your life, as it is not the complete picture of who you are meant to be in God's sight. What is it that you want to do with your life? Do not answer this question right away, as many people do not know how best to answer it. It may take some deep thought regarding your skill set, passions, and desires. If you are like me, there may be many things that you would like to accomplish, and it is difficult to pick one place to get started. The best thing is to consult God and get started charting your course.

Russell Simmons posted on Twitter in 2014 that "real richness lies in simply being happy with what you have, whether it's a lot, a little, or nothing at all."[7] Once you can focus on what truly matters, you can develop a plan for your future. You will then begin to move beyond living check to check and toward the real reason you are here.

LUST FOR MATERIAL THINGS

Our lust for material things contributes significantly to our aspirations for money. It creates an idol for us to seek out at all costs in hopes of building a seemingly better life. We desire earthly goods, only to leave them behind. Although I had fulfilled all my childhood earthly dreams by the age of thirty-two, I still felt as if there was more to attain.

---

7. Russell Simons, @uncleRush, Feb. 3, 2014.

There was still more missing from my life. I felt unfulfilled, and, by all accounts, I should have been completely satisfied with the life I had made for myself. Yet this was not enough, and my soul was not satisfied. I once dreamed of nice jewelry, a big house, a nice car, being able to travel around the world, and having access to millions of dollars. I have experienced most of those ambitious dreams to date—except for millions of dollars, as of this writing—yet my life was still yearning for something more.

There is more to our purpose. We need to understand what God has for us is bigger than anything this world can ever offer us. It is beyond anything your mind can imagine. I had to be completely out of work before I started to do the work of the Lord. This book is one of those efforts. Material things only satisfy the insatiable appetite that man has created for himself.

However, once you channel your lust for the material things of this world to a constant love for God, you will become full. You will no longer need the jewelry. Your desires will grow from having your own house to building houses for God's people in both a physical and spiritual sense. You will begin to share more of yourself for the betterment of mankind. Whatever you loved to help you achieve your accomplishments will soon change to spreading your newfound love to the masses. You will develop a mindset of caring about more than what money can buy for you, which is a distraction from what you can do for others. You will use your talents to bring about change in the world. It is difficult to grasp how much the world needs your gifts to become a better place. Your presence in the world may be needed to change the circumstances of someone else beyond material gain. You can have nice things, but sharing your gifts and blessings with the world is much more fulfilling.

LUST FOR MATERIAL WEALTH CREATES POVERTY

Poverty runs rampant throughout our world, and it will take everyone's effort to deal with it. The meek will indeed inherit the earth—and if we all do our part, the meek will not have to suffer for long before the earth is shared with all. Instead of focusing on how much money we can make, we should focus on how many people we can help. Your family is one starting point. However, take note that Jesus had to leave his home to show his glory and for it to be accepted.

Of course, you want to ensure that you are well taken care of during your retirement years, but also make sure that you are helping others who may have less than you along the way. The most giving people whom I have come across are those who generally have less to give. How many times do you think about the poor when you are lusting after your financial goals? There are so many opportunities to help those who are less fortunate in this country. According to a report for Feeding America, in 2014, over 46.7 million people (14.8 percent) were in poverty, and 15.5 million (21.1 percent) of children under the age of eighteen were in poverty.[8] These numbers reflect the impoverished people in our backyards whom we can help or assist.

However, these numbers pale in comparison to the global pandemic of hunger that is plaguing our world. Dosomething.org, the social change platform that encourages young people to take charge and create a campaign to drive change, states the following:

1. Nearly half of the world's population—more than three billion people—live on less than $2.50 a day. More than 1.3 billion live in extreme poverty—less than $1.25 a day.

2. One billion children worldwide are living in poverty. According to UNICEF, 22,000 children die each day due to poverty.

3. Worldwide, 805 million people do not have enough food to eat.[9]

These are things after which to lust. If you want to chase after something of importance, lust after things that matter. Chase your money to make a difference, not only in your life but in the lives of others as well. How many times have you been to Starbucks this week? How many times have you eaten out this week? How many times have you bought items you did not need? This is not an indictment of how you spend your money. You have earned it, and it is your right to buy what you want. This is just a comparison as to how an insignificant amount of money may mean nothing to you, but it may mean everything to someone else.

In other parts of the world, $2.50 a day makes a huge difference. The American panhandlers whom you come across every day, who take the spare change you give, would live like gods and goddesses in some of these areas. That homeless guy whom you pass every day on your way to work would be well off based on the living wages some people receive around the world. The world needs our help. When we consider that almost a million people die each year due to poverty and impoverished living conditions, how do we continue to ignore the world's cry out for help? This type of pain and hunger happens in America as well.

8. Weinfield et al., "Hunger in America 2014."
9. DoSomething.org, "Eleven Facts about World Hunger."

LOVE FOR MONEY OR GOD

Lustful wishes for money are tempting. The allure of what money can do for you and the doors it can open is attractive. However, that is fool's gold. I am sure you have heard the stories of millionaires who are miserable and are not happy with their lives. Money addresses only one issue in your life, financial stability. Money is a key asset within modern society, based on the values one has on his life, but money alone can never secure your joy.

However, more money tends to attract more bills, more family drama, and many other temptations that affect your happiness and your relationship with money. People soon learn that money does not comfort you, love you when it hurts, or tell you it will get better. But God does say these things to us. God is not interested in how much money you have. He is interested in your heart and what you will do with the money you have to help glorify his kingdom.

Several billionaires like Bill Gates, Warren Buffet, Michael Bloomberg, and many others have pledged to give away at least half of their fortune to a philanthropic cause, agreeing to what is being called the Giving Pledge. Making this effort a priority to them is derived from the goodness of their hearts, and it will be a blessing to those who are the recipients of the pledge. Yes, there is a massive tax write-off, but I have to believe there is more to it than that. Everyone listed on the pledge has made a significant amount of money. However, they made it a priority to take care of others with what they were blessed to obtain. Again, they cannot take the money with them when they die.

What is the point of being selfish, when God has opened doors for them, provided their companies with capable employees, and made them competent enough to achieve their varying levels of financial success? How could you be selfish and lust after only material things, when it is evident that the next step in success, as demonstrated by some of the world's most financially successful people, is to share with those who are less fortunate? Helping others should be the goal of each of us. Without the drive to help one another, achieving success does not mean anything to the purpose of heaven's calling. What God wants from us has nothing to do with our financial gain. His demands are completely different; he wants only you.

Challenge 4

Being Selfish

God Calls on Us to Give

The fourth challenge we are facing in America is simply being selfish. Although selfishness may seem like a harmless trait, its impact can be significant. You may think of being selfish as not being concerned about others or being mainly concerned for your own well-being above all else. However, selfishness typically has an adverse impact on other people. When you think of selfish motives as a corporate or global pursuit, the effect can be catastrophic.

From birth, we were taught and encouraged to share everything. Share with your siblings, share with your classmates, or share with your friends. We were graded on our ability to share as children. Teachers measure and grade sharing because it is an essential part of our becoming effective citizens in the world.

How do we expect to be given anything, if we are not able to give of ourselves? Acts 20:35 states, "In all things I have shown you that by working hard in this way we must help the weak and remember the words of the Lord Jesus, how he himself said, 'It is more blessed to give than to receive.'" This is not to say that we are Jesus or will be as selfless as Jesus, but we should strive to be more like him. In doing so, we should give more of ourselves. The phrase "it is better to give than to receive" is one we have all heard before, but how many of us implement this practice? We are in the age of receiving and wanting more attention. We want attention so badly that we will watch, record, and post someone suffering instead of helping the individual being harmed or wronged, just to entertain our followers. This is a form of selfishness and being inconsiderate.

The entire digital world has become a place of sharing, but how much is it affecting the conversation? We share on all social media platforms, whether we want to or not. Sharing is a pivotal part of who we are and what our society has become. Some of the largest organizations in the world base their business models on sharing. Yet we have neglected to share what matters. How did such a simple and important lesson from our childhood completely vanish by the time we became adults? Yes, we share digitally, but America's society seems to have taken a selfish approach to the idea of sharing, as an act of practicality. America has stopped sharing and has begun taking.

This form of taking is not just related to illegal criminal activity, although the feeling is remarkably similar to when someone steals from you. The legalized form of taking by societal constructs is just as threatening and hurtful. It is simply that no one can do anything about the stealing, since it is being done by corporate entities under laws that benefit only the corporation. What makes the corporate practice of being selfish and taking more egregious is that, many times, these organizations are not reprimanded for their practices. They prey on the poor and take advantage of those less fortunate while marketing themselves under the guise of support and help. Corporations such as student loans, financial security, insurance, healthcare, grocery stores, restaurants, and access to quality care are all guilty of selfish practices.

THE PLIGHT OF STUDENT LOANS

What do you do when student loans are your biggest expense? How do you combat this behemoth that hounds you for at least twenty years of your life? You went to college to educate yourself, because you were told this is the best way to secure a better future. However, college is expensive, and if you are from a poor background, paying for college is not a realistic option for your family. The next logical step for you is to borrow money from a student loan organization. This choice leaves you starting from the back of the pack.

These organizations seemingly target poor children in their marketing practices to keep their operations going. The poor are obviously the best customers for these loan companies. Wealthier families write checks per semester for their children to attend college. However, just like the payday loan industry, the student loan companies see the poor student as their next meal ticket. The relationship you have with a student loan company is mobbish, which means, if you do not have their money, they are coming after you with guns blazing. Student loan organizations can garnish your wages, ruin your credit, and take up to 15 percent of your social security and disability checks. The process of taking out a student loan would be fine if these companies were not so selfish and greedy. The interest terms are astronomical, and their payoff is worse than that of a mortgage.

As a student, you can borrow up to $80,000 or more to obtain your undergraduate and graduate degrees. If you are paying on your loan from the start, without missing a payment and exceeding your monthly payments, there is no reason your student loans should soar upwards of $200,000 with an initial $80,000 loan. But you spend thousands just to cover the interest, never making a dent in the principal of the loan. Car and mortgage loans are structured under much better terms than student loans. Except for the infamous five-year adjustable rate mortgage (ARM) program that helped to collapse the economy, I am not sure there is another loan structure worse than student loans. How are the operations of student loan companies completely legal? This societal drawback torments students nationwide and causes a great deal of undue stress and hardship. Meanwhile, many colleges abroad offer free advanced education to their citizens, yet Americans are suffering trying to make ends meet while paying on student loans.

Peter Thiel, serial entrepreneur and co-founder of PayPal, writes in his book *Zero to One*, "Higher education is the place where people who had big plans in high school get stuck in fierce rivalries with equally smart peers over conventional careers like management consulting and investment banking. For the privilege of being turned into conformists, students (or their families) pay hundreds of thousands of dollars in skyrocketing tuition that continues to outpace inflation."[1] How ridiculous is this concept of higher education under these circumstances? Peter Thiel is correct. You spend four years in school and end up with an unwanted companion in student loans that will be there harassing you for decades. Thiel then asks, "Why are we doing this to ourselves?" I pose the same question. Furthermore, why is our country allowing this type of racketeering to legally take place? The propaganda of higher education and the costs associated with it are ridiculous. Education should be a tool to better our society, but the key players who control the education industry can only selfishly see dollar signs.

Other industrialized countries pay for their citizens to attend college or offer some form of free education, but America extorts their families. The following is the college conundrum. You cannot get a well-paying job

---

1. Thiel with Masters, *Zero to One*, 36.

without a good college education. You cannot go to college without paying for it. You must pay the loan back with excessive interest that eats into your income that pays for your livelihood. You pay taxes on your income after you have graduated, while having a corrupt student loan bill with which to contend. All the while, you must figure out how to make a living.

This does not seem like a fair deal for a citizen of a country that cares about its people. This feels like you are receiving the short end of the stick. It seems as if the only way up the corporate ladder is to dig yourself into a deep hole, then try to climb out of it. If your family is financially less fortunate, the odds are not in your favor.

It appears as if you will be both uneducated and remain in poverty, or you will go to college and still struggle to make ends meet, because the entire system has its hands reaching into your pockets. This system contributes to the rat race, which leads to living paycheck to paycheck. There is no progress within this system. It will take you anywhere from ten (extremely expensive) years to twenty-five (still expensive) years to pay off your student loans. A lot of people die with that burden. The standard repayment plan for federal student loans puts borrowers on a ten-year track to pay off their debt. But research has shown the average bachelor's degree holder takes twenty-one years to pay off his or her loans. Under federal income-based repayment options, the remaining debt was forgiven after twenty years. You would have at least twenty years to pay off something that took you four years to acquire. However, President Trump and his office put an end to this program, so those who had hope about paying off their student loans are now hopeless. Your student loan is essentially a terrible mortgage on which you are upside down and cannot foreclose, nor can you sell or share.

Another unfortunate part of the student loan debacle is that you cannot live inside your degrees. You are probably renting your actual home because you cannot afford to buy a house, due to the cost of your education. Kanye West discusses the concept of degrees in his first album, *College Dropout*. His "School Spirit Skit 2" talks about the complication of obtaining a degree and the difficulty associated with being caught up in education and not figuring out how to make a living. This is a hilarious skit. However, the more you think about it, the sadder the situation becomes. The system is built against your success, and the poorer you are, the harder it is to succeed—even if you do everything everyone else did to succeed.

The *Huffington Post* ran an article by Cryn Johannsen that states, "Suicide is the dark side of the student lending crisis and, despite all the media attention to the issue of student loans, it's been severely under-reported."[2]

---

2. Johannsen, "The Ones We've Lost."

How does this issue continue to be swept under the rug as something that is completely tolerated? The housing market came crashing down due to an outrageous lending program; however, student loan companies are left to operate unscathed while people are suffering. Debt is very troubling, and it is killing us. Sara Routhier, an author from Loans.org, states, "The pathways to suicide can be influenced by many things: a history of depression, family loss, and a sense of loneliness, to name a few."[3]

Student loans create a profound despair of your livelihood. Many parents who have dealt with student loans try to ensure their children do not have to go down a similar path. They understand that it is unjust and stressful. As I will explain later, stress is a silent killer within America. Student loans help to contribute to that stress.

The Bible says a great deal about debt and lending money. However, Proverbs 22:7 says it best when it comes to student loans. Verse 7 reads, "The rich rules over the poor, and the borrower is the slave of the lender." When you borrow money for school, you truly feel as if you are a slave to the system. You begin to feel as if there is no way out, and your success is being hindered by student loans. You want to make it out of a check-to-check lifestyle, but student loans make it incredibly difficult to achieve this task. Something must change here. America must stop this practice of selfishness while preying on its citizens over the outlandish practices of student loan organizations.

Student loan schemes are just one of America's selfish behaviors. Food allocation, healthcare and healthcare costs, payday loans, the housing industry, and banking/investments are a few more of the unfortunate selfish situations with which Americans have to deal.

AMERICA'S INTERNAL VIEW

America is considered the greatest world power. We have the strongest military and will take any other country to task over America being the land of the free. However, with that freedom comes a great deal of hate and animosity, because Americans look at life from an intrinsic point of view. Many Americans believe our way is the right way to live and create selfish biases reflecting our views. We even hate different factions of people within our country. America has intense racial differences, which are primarily surmised on baseless ideologies. We also have Christians who use Christianity as a crutch to hate someone else's sin instead of reflecting on their own sin. As Jesus said, we are all hypocrites. It is not productive to center your lives around what you know or to what you are accustomed without

---

3. Routhier, "Living on the Edge."

being sympathetic to another person's experiences. Until you are out of your comfort zone and have a true interaction with someone of a different background, you will tend to judge people based on your limited knowledge and experience.

How can we love each other when there is so much selfishness within us? America is a melting pot of all the world's cultures. But our desire to not see each other as people instead of enemies creates a tumultuously unstable way to live. We may be different people, but our oneness is more important than any race, creed, religion, color, or sexual preference. We cannot allow our selfishness, lack of being accepting, and lovelessness to cloud our judgment toward mankind. These are issues we have to fix, because, if we do not, we will risk judgment coming from the heavenly Father. James 3:16 states, "For where jealousy and selfish ambition exist, there will be disorder and every vile practice."

The teen years of the twenty-first century have not been particularly productive when analyzing human interactions in this country. Selfishness has run rampant as different groups of people have created an us-vs.-them mentality. Black Lives Matter vs. Blue Lives Matter vs. White Lives Matter vs. All Lives Matter demonstrations have rooted themselves within the fabric of isolation among races and ideologies within this country, creating a sense of selfish hate for one another.

However, it is not that difficult to change our selfish ideas—or is it? A history that is as rich as ours in the philosophy of hate for one another purely based on skin color should be something that we can move past. But we can never seem to move forward. Perhaps we can begin by simply accepting those who are perceived to be different from us. We can also start to understand each other more by showing love to everyone—true agape love. Selfishness has no place to reside in people who give of themselves openly to others, without a desire to seek something in return.

WHAT DOES AMERICA'S RECORD SAY?

U.S. News ran a report on the overall best countries and listed some fascinating things about our beloved America. In 2016, when compared to other countries, America was ranked number four as the overall best country, behind Germany, Canada, and the UK.[4] In 2019, we slid to number eight. Each of these countries has fewer people, lower GDP, and lower GDP per capita. We were ranked number eleven on the citizenship category, stating that we are weak in trustworthiness. America is not trustworthy? What do

---

4. *U.S. News*, "Overall Best Countries Ranking."

you think may be contributing to this ranking? It must be the student loan system, or maybe it is the struggle of the poor, or perhaps it is our race relation problems that contribute to such a low score?

The report also states that we are overwhelmingly unhappy, resulting in a rating of three out of ten. Being overworked and not having a balanced life that focuses on positive relationships will keep us at a three or lower. We focus on so many things that contribute to this country's unhappiness. However, it is unfortunate to know that our country's unhappiness is reflected on a global scale. We make so much money, yet we are so unhappy. This ranking should put an end to the absurd question of whether money can buy happiness. We also received a 2.7 for safety and a 4.2 for a well-developed public health system. These two rankings are not hard to believe. You probably have had to deal with our baffling health care system, and feeling safe in America is not a reality for anyone, no matter where you live.

Americans love to kill each other, which makes it difficult to receive a high grade on the safety scale. Our first selfish response is to kill one another, instead of discussing differences and approaching each other with love.

Our capitalist mindset will keep our public health system low. We have good doctors—many of whom are here from other countries—but our inability to separate doing what is right from making a profit will keep our public health system ratings low. There are many books and topics of discussion referencing this issue of how health care is more about money than it is about keeping people healthy. Every component of our public health system plays a role in the disaster that is the US health structure. The government, hospitals, doctors, and pharmaceutical and insurance companies have a hand in our lacking public health system.

OUR COST OF WAR

On the other hand, America received high rankings for other items like power (our military strength), cultural influence, and entrepreneurship. These are things we cultivate and cherish. We push our cultural influence through entertainment. Hollywood dictates the perception of America, and our entertainment is how many countries learn about the US. Our military strength is obvious, and the leaders of this country will not let you forget it. The US still touts the mightiest military in the world and is happy to be boastful about it. This is where we place our fiscal obligations, thus ensuring our military might remain for years to come.

The report also states that, despite being the foremost global power, the US still faces domestic challenges, including racial tensions, income inequality, and an increasingly polarized electorate. While national security is a concern, so too is the debt incurred from wars meant to ensure it. While it is great that we have a strong military force, it is the unthinkably selfish motives by the leaders of this country to send soldiers to war over hapless and self-aggrandizing agendas that are in direct conflict with who we should be and for what we should stand as a country.

America has been involved in some form of war either directly or indirectly for most of its known existence as a country. The Centre for Research on Globalization published an article that stated that America has been at peace for only a total of twenty-one years since its birth. To put it in perspective, "since the United States was founded in 1776, she has been at war during 214 out of her 235 calendar years of existence."[5]

How do we ever expect the people of this country to stop hating and killing when this is all our country does worldwide? Hating and killing are seemingly key characteristics of this country. Of course, we are listed highly as a military power; we have been training throughout our entire existence for combat. The Centre's article also points out more distressing information about America and our tendency to fight. If we pick any year since 1776, "there is about a 91 percent chance that America was involved in some war during that calendar year." Think about that statistic: we have been killing since birth.

According to an article on the US wars written by Megan Crigger and Laura Santhanam of PBS, "Over 1.1 million Americans have died in all U.S. wars."[6] These are the recorded numbers of soldiers who have perished for our country's or our allies' interests. Countless others have been lost at war or are missing in action. We also have people suffering long-term mental and physical effects from warfare as well. Looking after veterans should be more than a political talking point.

INTERNALIZED BLOODLUST

Our fascination with killing and the battle scars we have gained shows that it is no coincidence the US leads the developed world in deaths due to firearms. This is the culmination of selfishness. How do you hope for peace in a country that does not know peace? How do you hope for love in a country that does not know love? How do we stop killing each other, when our country has been nothing more than a killing machine since it was founded?

    5. Washington's Blog and Global Research, "America Has Been at War."
    6. Crigger and Santhanam, "How Many Americans Have Died."

It is just like America to perform well on all the financial aspects of a global ranking system but to falter mightily in social welfare rankings. We struggle in the thing about which God cares most: love and relationships. We must be able to keep our core values while strengthening our relationships with one another.

Our internalized viewpoint of America shows us a narrow scope of the world and builds on our selfish nature. Yes, America may be a good country with a decent democratic process; however, we cannot allow our self-centered point of view to enable us to continue killing with complete disregard toward the betterment of the world. Both foreign and domestic wars are still wars, where casualties are sure to rise. The matter of killing each other is not an issue where you would need to be a Rhodes scholar of the Bible to understand that "thou shall not kill" is not only a basic principle of God but should be a basic principle of being human. Yet we fail God each day by showing how unworthy we are to even begin considering the concept of loving one another. Where do we begin to right our wrongs?

AMERICA'S HOMELESSNESS

America, as great as she is, has a homeless problem. Homelessness is one of the most unbelievable ways this country shows how selfish it is. According to the National Alliance to End Homelessness, "there were over 500,000 homeless people in the US in January 2015." The statistics below help to paint a picture of how dire the homeless problem is in America:

- In January 2015, 564,708 people were homeless on any given night in the United States.
- Of that number, 206,286 were people in families, and
- 358,422 were individuals.
- About 8 percent of homeless people—47,725—are veterans.[7]

Homelessness should be a non-issue in America. Instead of the US spending upwards of $350 million to build a new F22 fighter jet, we can allocate those funds to eradicate the homelessness of 47,725 veterans. It is quite selfish for the leaders of this country to ask veterans, many of whom come from poor or underprivileged areas, to commit the ultimate sacrifice for their country. Then when they come home, these veterans are not well taken care of. Veteran homelessness should be nonexistent in America. It is

7. National Alliance to End Homelessness, "Homelessness in America."

complete and utter nonsense for a country that prides itself on the might of its military to shun the people who make this military mighty.

This country should also be able to take on the issue of the chronically homeless as well, for veterans and everyone else. The American government spends billions on programs and agendas that do not matter. For example, in 2013, the federal government spent over $432 million on warplanes that will not be used, ever.[8] Politicians continuously raise obscene amounts of money to be elected for office. Each year the price to become an elected official seems to increase. We are continuously bombarded by political conversations. We never give thought to some of those millions of dollars that are spent to get their messages in front of us can be spent doing good within our homeless population.

What happens to the money provided to the politicians that lose the election? Before 1989 politicians used to spend it, but now they cannot use the monies for personal use. However, what if the politicians would use whatever funds that are available after an election to help end America's homelessness. Afterall, most of that money is being raised by the people of America. This country is too powerful to have an issue like homelessness continue. Philippians 2:3–4 encourages us to "do nothing from rivalry or conceit, but in humility count others more significant than yourselves. Let each of you look not only to his own interests, but also to the interests of others."

HOMELESSNESS PERSISTS

America often looks out for its interest, sending millions of dollars of aid to other countries. Yet we have at least 500,000 people who need a home. We must be able to look at the homeless population and understand that there needs to be a system in place to help. Even the criminals in this country have a place to stay. Some people would rather commit crimes in order to have a place to sleep at night instead of being on the streets, especially during the winter months. According to the National Healthcare for the Homeless Council, "For every age group, homeless persons are three times more likely to die than the general population." This is senseless when you factor in the wealth of this country. The report also states, "The average age of death of homeless persons is about fifty years, the age at which Americans commonly died in 1900."[9]

8. Giokaris, "Twenty Ridiculous Ways."
9. National Health Care for the Homeless Council, "Fact Sheets."

We all must consider this rate of mortality to be abhorrent within our country. Homeless people are at a higher risk for illness as well, at rates three to six times higher than the general population. This includes diseases such as HIV/AIDS, tuberculosis, and influenza, as well as cancer, heart disease, diabetes, and hypertension.

Not only do the homeless people of America have to deal with severe health issues without any appropriate recourse, but "seventy-one cities across the country passed or tried to pass ordinances that criminalize feeding homeless people," according to Michael Stoops, director of community organizing at the National Coalition for the Homeless.[10] It is unfortunate states are pushing to eliminate feeding the homeless. Stoops mentions, "The uptick in food-sharing restrictions is driven in part by what cities perceive to be the rising visibility of the homeless." The message we are sending is far off base from what the gospel of the Lord preaches about how we are to treat those who have less than we do. Stoops says, "Cities have grown tired of the problem, so they think by criminalizing homelessness they'll get rid of the visible homeless populations." Our priorities are so wrong in America and completely off base with the principles of Christianity.

How ridiculous is the idea of criminalizing homelessness? These cities neglect to understand that anyone can run into an issue that may cause a financial setback. The number of cities trying to pass these so-called feeding bans is on the rise, Stoops comments. American cities would let the homeless population starve in this country, because it is a cheaper alternative than feeding them or helping them. How could the leadership of these cities adhere to this careless ideology that homeless people are unsightly? What about stepping in to help support the homeless? The idea of forcing homeless people away instead of finding a solution to help address the issues that may be plaguing them is unconscionable.

In 2014, the United Nations Human Rights Committee criticized the United States for the criminalization of homelessness, noting that such "cruel, inhuman and degrading treatment is in violation of international human rights treaty obligations."[11] There should be no division over this issue, and the fact that we have laws criminalizing human struggle is ludicrous. How can we call ourselves a great nation when we allow laws like these to be passed or even thought of within this country? Why does it take a response from the United Nations to prompt action? Should the leaders of America be able to see how cruel this treatment is to those who are severely disadvantaged?

10. Stoops, ed., "Food-Sharing Report."
11. Levintova, "Is Giving Food."

Proverbs 22:16 states, "Whoever oppresses the poor to increase his own wealth, or gives to the rich, will only come to poverty." This country tends to cater to the rich. America is a Christian country that is also home to many other religions and faiths. However, the thing that we do best is to omit many Christian values. America oppresses the poor and makes them feel insignificant for being poor. Ezekiel 7:19 says, "They cast their silver into the streets, and their gold is like an unclean thing. Their silver and gold are not able to deliver them in the day of the wrath of the LORD. They cannot satisfy their hunger or fill their stomachs with it. For it was the stumbling block of their iniquity." These words sum up the gist of human behavior and the endless lust for money. We have historically allowed money to dictate the decisions this country makes. However, when it comes to basic human decency, money should be secondary. But as America revolves around a baseless and unquenchable thirst for money, hundreds of thousands of people are sitting alongside the streets thrown aside like worthless waste.

All the money in the world will not save you from illness. Money will not save you from death. Money can save people from homelessness, but we are allocating our funds elsewhere. The only thing that America seems to value is capitalism, and it just may be killing us, especially the homeless. For the sake of those who are less fortunate, let us value life and end homelessness once and for all.

SELFISHNESS IMPACTS PUERTO RICO

America protects the needs of other countries and helps to stabilize governments been affected by war, but what about the citizens of its own country who wish to get back on their feet? We can look at our response to our territory of Puerto Rico to see how selfish this country can be. In September 2017, Hurricane Maria pounded Puerto Rico and left the island devastated.

Our country's response was a failure. There were as many as 2,975 deaths and many people were left homeless due to that disaster. Congress approved $20 billion to help Puerto Rico recover from Hurricane Maria in 2017. As of March 1, 2019, less than $14,000 of the $20 billion approved by Congress had been spent on post-disaster reconstruction activities in Puerto Rico, according to the Department of Housing and Urban Development records.[12] We can do better than this. We must do better than this.

---

12. Madrid, "With Hurricane Season Looming."

RELIGIOUS SEPARATION

We must work to create a less selfish world, instead of believing someone or something is better than someone or something else. For instance, thinking you worship God better than someone else worships God, your love is better than another person's love, your race is better than another race, or the wealth you have accumulated makes you better than someone else are all determinates of separation and segregation. When I look at God's love, even as a passive observer of the many religious beliefs on earth, there is an appreciation in knowing he made us all the same.

We should not use symbols or statuses as a way to separate ourselves, because we are all going through the same thing, just in our own ways and from our own perspectives. How can we go about creating change in the world if we refuse to see the world from another person's perspective? It takes a great deal of openness and growth to understand that we are the same and are experiencing the challenges of life just like everyone else. Perhaps we are lost and looking for a way to identify with each other. Maybe we cannot fully grasp the concept that we are all humans, living on earth, simply trying to survive. If we all feel trapped, it would help explain why we are completely missing the mark and are lashing out at others.

Today, America and the West are at war with the Islamic State of Iraq and Syria (ISIS) or people who have been politicized as radical Islamists. Islam is a religion just like Christianity. It is not to be demonized. However, we tend to forget that their children are just like our children. They are young, impressionable, and completely held captive to the beliefs of their parents while venturing into a world of unknowns. Parents teach their children what to think; therefore, prejudiced behavior is manmade. It is a construct of man to create a separation of religious ideology and turn it into hatred. This hatred stems from selfishness or looking at life from one point of view.

JESUS, MUHAMMAD, OR ABRAHAM

Jesus, Muhammad, and Abraham all believed there is a higher power that reigns supreme over everyone. It does not matter how they referred to him when they called out for God, Allah, HaShem Adonai, or YHWH. God is known by many names. According to the Bible, he also changed our tongues at the city of Babel, so is it farfetched that people were sent different leaders whom God deemed were the best fit for their culture to deliver his ultimate message?

This may or may not be the case; I am not sure. I do know, however, that people go to war and kill each other over these religious fathers or religious ideologies. However, most religious leaders only seek love for their people and their followers. First John 4:12 states, "No one has ever seen God; if we love one another, God abides in us and his love is perfected in us." All God wants is for us to love without reservation? How many people must perish before we stop pursuing our false ambitions? Our religious fathers revered God. On a trip to China, I even saw a large Buddha statue pointing up and down, seemingly acknowledging a greater power—although, as far as I know, Buddhists do not believe in one deity.

Yes, the Bible, Qur'an, Torah, and other religious books speak of great battles in the name of their God, but God had the final say. We must understand that our religious preferences have a lot to do with our surroundings and should not be predicated on hate. However, our selfish ambitions encourage us to take judgment into our own hands.

This judge, jury, and executioner mindset we have adopted is a flawed system. It will ultimately fail, as God does not abide by our rules or our understanding. I am a Christian, but perhaps that is because I was raised as a Christian. If I had been raised in another part of the world, my religion may have been something else. We tend to become and believe what we are taught as children. We follow the guidance of the leaders within our enclosed community to develop an understanding of who we are in the world and what we believe. We must step outside of ourselves and establish a foundation of tolerance within the institution of religion, because it appears as if this key component of mankind, which is designed to keep us together, is easily pulling us apart.

LIVES LOST DUE TO RELIGION

Whether or not you believe in dinosaurs, evolution, or Adam and Eve, history tells a similar fate for earth's inhabitants. The Christian faith and scientific postulation—both say the end of earth for its inhabitants will be comprised of a terrible death. We can waste our time here being selfish if we desire, but God has the final say. Regardless if existence ends because of a meteor or an asteroid, forty days and nights of rain, fire and brimstone, or the absolute extinguishing of life because of an exploding star, the planet Earth as we know it is believed to face certain death. Why should we waste these precious moments in time being selfish and hating each other? We have only now to love and appreciate each other. We can make this world what God would like for it to be, a creation of which he can be proud.

Religious wars have been fought possibly since before we started understanding the concept of time, and, unfortunately, they continue to this day. And it is all in the name of God, right? Most religions teach peace and what it means to love, yet we fight each other over whose peace is best. I am at a loss in understanding the reason behind religious wars, but these wars are often the bloodiest, because they are filled with the most passion.

AddictiveLists.com lists some of the largest religious battles in world history, including the Second War of Kappel (700 people died), Lebanese Civil War (150,000 people died), the Crusades (more than half a million civilians died), the Second Sudanese Civil War (two million people died), the First Sudanese Civil War (500,000 people died), the Great Peasant Revolt (200,000 people died), the Nigerian Civil War (more than one million people died), and there were the Thirty and Eighty Years wars as well.[13] These numbers do not include the Holocaust or World War II, where over six million Jewish people were killed at the orders of Nazi rule. The Holocaust is also known as a genocide. However, when the intent is to kill all the people of Jewish faith, it is fair to consider the Holocaust a religious war. These listed wars did not happen on US soil, and we were involved only in World War II. However, these religious wars are the price we pay for infusing our humanistic ideas with misinterpretations of biblical principles. In America, slave owners would use the Bible to control and make unfounded laws to impact the lives of slaves.

The current war with the Islamic State of Iraq and the Levant (ISIL) is also a loosely based religious war taking its toll on thousands of people today. ISIL does not represent the entire religion of the Muslim faith. Crigger and Santhanam recorded how wars have impacted Americans with their article "How Many Americans Have Died in U.S. Wars?" Their research shows that over 1.1 million Americans have died in all US wars. Our current War on Terror against ISIL, ISIS, and other groups has taken about 7,000 American lives as of this writing.[14] Although the Old Testament is filled with religious wars, the New Testament speaks about loving our enemy and loving one another. The method of the New Testament, when it concerns peace, seems to be the best way to deal with the differences for spiritual people like me.

A CALL TO END SELFISHNESS

We must end the selfish mindset and get to know one another. The social determinates that have stemmed from this type of behavior have allowed

---

13. AddictiveLists.com, "Religious Wars."
14. Crigger and Santhanam, "How Many Americans Have Died."

us to idly standby and watch our brethren suffer. We should seek to completely end homelessness and, at the very least, create a path to eradicate homelessness within the veteran population. We must also stop hate based on religion, because love knows no limits, even within the confines of our dogmatic beliefs. This country should no longer allow the capitalist mindset of outrageous student loans to cripple society and impede the progress of its citizens now and for future generations.

The next step in evolution is simple. However, it will take extraordinary and collective power to evolve from our current barbaric existence to a magnificent force that will radiate with understanding and appreciation of one another.

John 15:12–14 states, "This is my commandment, that you love one another as I have loved you. Greater love has no one than this, that someone lay down his life for his friends. You are my friends if you do what I command you." These are the words that God has left for us by which to abide—no more being selfish or self-centered with our negative thinking about one another. Instead, we should embrace each other's differences and celebrate them, because we can sympathize with each other's pain and glory. The story that made you who you are is like the stories of many others.

All religions should worship freely and show love and respect to each other. Ultimately, it does not matter where you pray or whom you call Lord if you identify each other as brother. God will be the judge of whether we have it right or wrong. There is no reason for me to hate you because you wear a hijab or pray to Allah. There is no reason for you to hate me because I believe in Jesus Christ. And there is no reason for me to show a lack of tolerance or hate people because they believe Abraham is the way.

Our religious beliefs are a part of who we are, but they are only a part. We have so much more in common as people. And every time we greet each other, tolerance, caring, empathy, and love should emit from our souls. Our time on earth is short in the grand scheme of eons, so why not make the most out of it? Let us walk with each other instead of squaring off against each other. What good are we doing if we are harming each other in the name of peace? God offers infallible love to us all; we should get rid of our selfish indulgence and thought processes to offer each other love just the same.

Challenge 5

Being Stressed

We Cannot Allow the Stressors of Life to Live Life for Us

Stress is difficult to avoid. It is easy to imagine but harder to fully understand its impact on your life. I am sure you have all dealt with the challenge of stress in some form within your life. Stress could be derived from a variety of factors. Perhaps it is your job, your children, your spouse, money issues, or the lack of love (either from yourself or others) that is causing you this unnecessary strain. Stress is more than having a bad day; we all have those. Stress builds up and places extra pressure on you. Sometimes stress can be so heavy that you can feel it weighing you down. Stress is such a contaminate within our lives that an organization, the American Institute of Stress, was founded to address its compounding issues. We throw around the phrase "I am stressed out" oftentimes in a jovial manner, but stress is a real epidemic that needs to be seriously addressed.

Effectively confronting stress is an important component of successfully managing your life. Stress contributes to many health-related complications. Too much of it can lead to chest pain, heartburn, or headaches in some people. Stress can become so intense that people do not want to get out of bed. They would rather lie down all day instead of facing their stress triggers. Hans Selye, the man who coined the term *stress*, studied it and its symptoms for years.[1]

---

1. American Institute of Stress, "What Is Stress?"

He also believed there is good stress or *eustress*, which is stress or pressure that is used to help you perform better. For example, the rush of emotion that may overcome people before a performance is considered eustress. However, when any stress becomes too much to bear, your body reacts negatively.

Studies have shown that if you are already afflicted with diseases or conditions like obesity, heart disease, Alzheimer's disease, diabetes, depression, gastrointestinal problems, or asthma, adding stress is a recipe for disaster. I believe it is of the utmost importance for people to identify stress and find out how to cure or address their stressors in a productive manner. Your solution may include the need for professional help, but I have found that having a faith-based relationship with God can help you combat any stress-related issues as well.

To provide more context in explaining how high a priority that managing stress needs to be in your life, R. Morgan Griffin wrote an article in which he lists the top ten health problems related to stress.[2] The first health problem is heart disease. Heart disease runs rampant within this country and can be attributed to several factors. However, adding stress to the mix of someone who is suffering from heart disease can be deadly. Many people die daily due to heart disease. How many of them are dying due to the compounding factor of unnecessary stress?

The second health problem identified is asthma. Griffin finds that many studies have shown that stress can worsen asthma. He states "that some evidence suggests that a parent's chronic stress might even increase the risk of developing asthma in their children." Passing asthma down as a generational illness because of the increase in stress seems to be a manageable condition for the parents. Overcoming stress is not only important to us as parents, but research is telling us that we should reduce stress for the sake of our unborn children as well. The constructs of life can create situations that are not advantageous for us in which to succeed or live a stress-free life; however, we have the power to tackle stress early on and reduce the risk of our children developing asthma. The stress with which you are dealing can become a generational issue for your children.

The third health issue is obesity, where people with high levels of stress seem to store more fat in the belly, which apparently poses greater health risks than fat on the legs or hips. We try to eat away or sleep away our stressors. We even stress over the fact that we are stressing out. Pointless eating, sleeping, and stressing culminates in excessive weight gain and obesity. Obesity is the culprit behind many of life's ailments. When we factor in stress, obesity can easily be exacerbated. Americans leads the world in

---

2. Griffin, "Ten Health Problems."

obesity or being at-risk for obesity, which potentially corresponds to the level of stress with which we are dealing in this country.

The fourth health ailment is diabetes. Griffin states, "Stress can worsen diabetes in two ways. First, it increases the likelihood of bad behaviors, such as unhealthy eating and excessive drinking. Second, stress seems to raise the glucose levels of people with type 2 diabetes directly." The more we allow stress to control our lives, the less we are in control of our health. Diabetes is manageable, but when stress is added to the list of issues with which a diabetic must deal, the disease may have already won. I have had personal encounters with diabetes and stress plaguing my mother. Do not allow the two to ruin the joys of life for which God is preparing you.

The fifth health issue related to stress is headaches. We tend to think our headaches may be related to a cold, allergies, or some other illness, but stress may be the ultimate offender. The next time you have a headache or a migraine, think about what you could be stressing you and address that issue. Stress is typically the underlying condition of many other health conditions. Address what is stressing you out, and you may address the issue with your headache.

The sixth health issue is depression and anxiety. God says for us not to worry about anything. As his children, we are all taken care of, if we obey his commands. Our obedience and understanding of our relationship with God will rectify our bouts with depression and the need to feel anxious. Do not be anxious for anything, since all things will reveal themselves in due time and according to God's will and purpose for your life.

The seventh health-related issue is gastrointestinal problems. Many people can attest to the fact that stress can make ulcers worse and is also a common factor in many other GI conditions. You can see the pattern here.

If we have stress in our lives, everything else we are facing is exacerbated. There have been accounts where people have received a life-changing diagnosis, and it is remarkable how their outcomes are impacted based on the level of worry or stress they have. Those who stress less tend to live longer. For those who live a more stressful life, their conditions tend to worsen, and their bodies deteriorate faster.

My aunt had a bout with cancer and had to undergo chemotherapy for months. She did not always have a sure ride to her treatments and had other issues going on, including financial hardships. However, every time I called her, she was optimistic and positive about life. Instead of losing weight and her hair during chemotherapy, she gained a little weight and did not lose any of her hair. The doctors were surprised by how well she was responding to the treatments. After her regimen of treatments, she was cancer-free and has since been able to reduce her medications. She did not allow such an incredibly stressful experience to stress her out. She approached the matter with joy, optimism, and faith that God would pull her through.

The eighth health ailment related to stress is Alzheimer's disease. One animal study found that stress might worsen Alzheimer's disease, causing brain lesions to form more quickly. As my previous comments indicated, compounding stress is a comorbidity to any ailment and can prove to be detrimental to our chemical makeup. The brain is fragile, and we may forget things by ourselves; we do not need stress to speed up the process of aging or help with contracting a debilitating disease like Alzheimer's. The aggregation of stress leads to the deterioration of the human body and mind.

Accelerated aging is the ninth health issue. According to Griffin, "One study compared the DNA of mothers who were under high stress—they were caring for a chronically ill child—with women who were not. Researchers found that a region of the chromosomes showed the effects of accelerated aging. Stress seemed to accelerate aging about nine to seventeen additional years." I can imagine that the stress of having to raise a child or care for a loved one with a health condition can cause rapid aging. I have come across people who may be having a hard time with life or who are stressed out over certain issues who appeared to look much older than they were. It is probably best to not ask questions about an individual's age; just know that stress adds wrinkles and time to your body. Aging about nine to seventeen years is taking years away from your life. An example of accelerated aging due to stress can be seen in America's recent presidents. Each one, including Bill Clinton, George Bush, and Barack Obama, vacated the position looking like he had spent a lifetime in office. Personally, I had a head of wavy black hair before my children; now I am gray and bald.

Premature death is the tenth and most unfortunate health issue related to stress. A study cited by Griffin looked at the health effects of stress by studying elderly caregivers looking after their spouses—people who are naturally under a great deal of stress. It found that caregivers had a 63 percent higher rate of death than people their age who were not caregivers. This stat is affected by many factors, including being elderly and losing a loved one. People often attribute having a broken heart to the cause of death, but it is possibly the stress of dealing with the death of someone close that may have caused the caregiver's passing. According to Healthsystemtracker.org, the US leads or is in the top ranking of wealthy nations with a high rate of premature deaths.[3] The American lifestyle is taking a toll on us, but God has an answer, if we dare to follow his guide.

---

3. Kurani, "How Does the Quality."

MY BOUTS WITH STRESS

I have personal accounts of most of these diseases or conditions. Many of my immediate family members dealt with varying levels of stress as they struggled with the hardships of life. My mother developed gestational diabetes during her pregnancy with my sister. My mother tried to manage it, but after my sister died from cancer at the age of three, managing her diabetes became harder to do. I could tell that she was trying to improve her health, but burying your child is something no parent should have to do, especially when the child was such a young age.

The death of my sister took an unbearable toll on my mother for subsequent years. She stuck with me for another nine years after my sister's passing, but I am certain the stress of losing my sister never gave her rest. Burying your child is a difficult burden to carry.

I consider myself fortunate that my mother was able to see me graduate from college; however, she died the following year due to complications from diabetes at the age of only forty-two. It is difficult for me to understand the endless trials my mother faced. The moments of emptiness must have felt endless after my sister died. I do not believe she ever escaped the emotional stress and subsequent bouts of depression after losing my sister. Stress without an appropriate outlet or a source of comfort can take everything from you, especially if you feel as if you are traveling life's journey alone.

My mother went through several health-related issues from the previous list of stress complications, which, I believe, contributed to depression and premature death. It took years for me to regain my purpose in life after losing my mother. If God had not guided my life—by connecting me to the woman who would later become my wife—I honestly do not know where I would be.

I was young and living my life with the aspirations of making my mother's life better. I had the same dreams that many other young children from impoverished neighborhoods have. When you live in an environment where you see your family struggling to make it, your ambition drives you to succeed, or at least you develop the grit to doing more financially. I was determined to find my way out of poverty somehow, as well as to help my mother get through her difficulties. I thought about selling drugs, rapping, or finding some other means to make money, so that we did not have to worry about the financial challenges of life any longer.

However, God had other plans. As previously mentioned, I had a relationship with God. But just like any relationship, you can have a strain that shakes the foundation of your togetherness. The stress that I was under after losing my grandmother when she was sixty-five, a year after my sister was born, then losing my sister two years later, was a lot to deal with as a little boy. Finally, losing my mom a year after I graduated from college and a year before my wedding was truly enough to crush my spirit and the essence of my faith. The ebb and flow of happiness is a tough thing to deal with. I was going through my bouts with whatever happiness was at that time, because joy was the farthest thing from my mind.

It was a difficult time for me. I wanted to give up. But for some reason, not then known to me, I could not give up. Something would not let me break. My wife was also extremely supportive during the time of my mother's passing, and I could never thank her enough for her encouragement. At that point, she had never lost anyone close to her. Therefore, she could only console me but not fully empathize with the pain I felt, dealing with so much death as a young man.

So, I kept going back to God. I constantly asked the question of why for years. There were certainly moments when the only person to whom I thought I could relate was the biblical character Job. In Job 7:20, Job went to God to vent his frustrations and complain how his life was extremely difficult. God took everything away from Job just to show Satan that Job would be faithful regardless of his earthly possessions and accomplishments, including if Satan took the lives of his loved ones. I did not know the story of Job when I was going through my turmoil, but I can certainly empathize with Job after looking back at my circumstances.

The silent screams of pain, loneliness, and bitter sadness seemed determined to tear me apart. I repeatedly questioned God, trying to gain a better understanding of his purpose behind my loss. Just like Job, I pleaded with God. Job would say, "Why won't you leave me alone, at least long enough for me to swallow?" I could easily relate to that feeling of despair. It felt like living was too much to bear, and my future was unnervingly bleak. Again, like Job, I wondered why God would make me his target. What had I done that was so bad in the sight of God that I had to lose all the essential women in my life?

My heartbreak manifested itself in stress, as I knew I was no longer able to call my mother every night at 10 p.m. That feeling still haunts me. She was my best friend, and she is no longer there for me to call and discuss the happenings of my life. Even as my family was growing and I was gaining more reasons to love, the thought of all I had gone through was an excruciating process.

But then something happened. I am not sure what it was or why it occurred. I would cry some nights in my dreams. I dreamed I was talking to my mother, or I would find her in the house where she died, lying the exact way it was described to me when she was discovered by my relatives.

Even within the scenes of my dreams where she was alive, she would leave the room or vanish, and I would soon realize in my dream that she had died. This led me to cry in my dreams repeatedly. Over time, although these dreams were seemingly strange, they began to bring a little comfort. However, the stress of not having my mother was still weighing on my heart.

I began to talk with God a little more and learn about the situations people in the Bible faced. I read the Bible, not just for the sake of saying I was reading the Bible. I read the Bible for insight and to be uplifted. I read to better understand how to deal with stressful situations, like losing everything you hold dear and discovering God's true purpose for your life. The purpose you believe to be yours or ordained by God is not always the path that God has for you. I learned that sometimes you must go through tribulations and circumstances to see God begin to move in your life—because if it were not for those tribulations, you might not believe God is the one directing your path. Sometimes your faith has to be tested; otherwise, is it true faith?

I knew I desired a relationship with God. I needed to talk to him more and listen to him as well. It is not just a one-way street. I talked to God ad nauseam about my feelings. I began to develop a better relationship with him that allowed me to find a way out of my emotional distress. Both my mother and my sister died at young ages (forty-two and three). My grandmother died at sixty-five, and, unfortunately, that is a long time for many southern black people. Instead of dwelling on the thought of not having them in my life any longer, I began to appreciate the time I had spent with them.

God also filled my emptiness with three beautiful women: my wife and two daughters. It seemed as if I had lost three lovely women and gained three more in return. I have now been given a different mission and a different purpose. I no longer need to stress over the loss of my mother. I can find joy in the fact that she is no longer in the hospital with IVs strapped to her arms anytime she did not remember to take her insulin or neglected to eat enough food to counter the additional insulin intake. She was no longer suffering from any of the additional ailments that diabetes can cause, like amputation or loss of sight. My sister was no longer dealing with the perils of cancer anymore either. Managing my bouts with stress became easier when I learned to give God my stress.

THE TOLL OF STRESS

Stress has no place in your heart, which is why it causes discomfort. Deborah Hartz-Seeley wrote an article stating, "Chronic stress is linked to the six leading causes of death: heart disease, cancer, lung ailments, accidents, cirrhosis of the liver, and suicide."[4] This book could have been written about stress alone and potentially cover each of the seven challenges we are facing in America. The World Health Organization calls stress the health epidemic of the twenty-first century.[5] Of all the challenges we are facing in America, stress is the leading indicator of healthcare issues. According to the National Institute for Occupational Safety and Health, the workplace is the number one cause of stress. It also states that 110 million people die every year as a direct result of stress—seven people every two seconds.[6]

Stress kills more people than anything else. Stress does not belong in your body, mind, or spirit. There are several self-encouraging steps you can take to help mitigate any stress you may be feeling. You can do simple things like take deep breaths or breathe slowly to control your heart rate. You can break up your large tasks into smaller ones, which will help better manage your responsibilities. You can tell someone you are sorry or accept another person's apology to ease the burden and tension you may be feeling. We can learn to speak nicely to one another and smile a little more. Each of these may be considered a step to help you manage any stress you may be facing. There are several other things you can do like exercise, take a bath, or just simply find time to relax. And if you cannot manage stress by yourself, seek professional and spiritual help: let go and let God.

I have found that God's remedy has never failed me. When I lost my job; when we had miscarriages; when I went to the doctor on two separate occasions for unknown chest pain, thinking I was having some sort of heart ailment (which would have been rare for a relatively healthy young man in his late twenties and early thirties), I learned to lean on God even more. The more pressure under which you live, the more you learn to lean on God. I rely on God for tasks as routine as driving to work, because not everyone who drives to work make it home each day. Do not take one second for granted, and trust God to be there when you need him most.

Life can become overwhelming, especially when there is seemingly so much to do. You begin to lose your composure, and the structure of your life becomes undone. Even though my life felt like it was unraveling, I knew God would carry me beyond any hardships I could not handle on my own. During the storm (as religious people would put it), good things were happening every day.

For example, when I lost my job, we began receiving checks from unaccounted places. There were class-action lawsuits, mortgage overpayments,

---

4. Hartz-Seeley, "Chronic Stress Is Linked."
5. Soleil, "Workplace Stress."
6. CDC, "Stress . . . at Work."

escrow payments, and many other avenues of financial infusions that were supplying us with checks being deposited directly into our bank accounts when we needed them most. I am not saying to count on these things, as I believe we were fortunate, and these blessings were timely. However, I urge you to try God during your season of stress, and he will be there.

He made provisions for us to be blessed with two lovely girls after having a few miscarriages. My chest pain was proven to be nothing more than work tension and the ergonomics of my workstation. The job I lost afforded me the opportunity to do the Lord's work. I began to discover how to live my life on purpose and not just live for the sake of work. Do not stress your job, do not stress your relationships, and do not stress the day-to-day trials and tribulations. God is there, and he is waiting for you to tell him all about your troubles. He wants you to lean on him and not stress over things that you cannot change. He wants you to give your worries to him. I urge you to seriously give God a try when stress arises and become a witness to the power of faith in heavenly works.

GIVE GOD YOUR STRESS

Dealing with stress and depression—especially when you do not understand what God is doing at the time—is when you will find that God is most present. You must trust and believe that God knows what he is doing with absolute certainty. Although you may not see it or understand it while it is happening, trust that God will not give you more than you can handle.

In order to be a functional person, I had to learn how to better manage stress. That is not to say that life does not become stressful or that you will no longer have issues that get under your skin. Surely, life is still life, but God can help you overcome anything with which you are dealing. The following Scriptures will help you to gain a better appreciation for the love that God has for you, especially when dealing with stressful times. In the case of stress from other people, Psalm 118:5–6 states, "Out of my distress I called on the LORD; the LORD answered me and set me free. The LORD is on my side; I will not fear. What can man do to me?"

There is nothing man can do to you if God is with you. Everything on this earth is temporary, even a broken relationship with a significant other. God's love will grant you the protection you need so that you do not need to fear anything. Work, finances, relationship drama—all are under the protection of God's love. For those with heavy burdens, Psalm 55:22 states, "Cast your burden on the LORD, and he will sustain you; he will never permit the righteous to be moved." As someone who trusts God, I give him all that troubles me, so that I can be strengthened in my time of weakness. Just as he helped me through a tough period with the passing of my family members, God will help you face any burden that may come your way.

Many people face anxiety or uncertainty in their lifetimes. However, God does not want you to stress over any of life challenges. Philippians 4:6 instructs us by stating, "Do not be anxious about anything, but in everything by prayer and supplication with thanksgiving let your requests be made known to God." Tell God about your anxiety, stress, or anything you are having difficulty getting through. Then move as God instructs you to move without fear and with absolute and undoubted faith. Undoubted faith is a difficult skill to acquire, but once you can give it all to God without worry, the transformation is miraculous.

Challenge 6

Being Lazy

The sluggard does not plow in the autumn; he will seek at harvest and have nothing.

Proverbs 20:4

The idea of laziness is one of the most effortless states in which to indulge, yet it is one of the most difficult challenges to address. Being lazy is not merely discussing the topic of someone taking a day off or sleeping all day because of the energy spent working on a project. I know people who will feel as if they are being lazy for sleeping eight hours, after working a twelve-hour day, believing they could be doing something more productive.

Getting the proper amount of sleep or resting an appropriate amount of time is not considered lazy. Obtaining the correct amount of rest is a mandate by God, which is why our bodies become dysfunctional when we do not get enough rest. At work, the two o'clock drag usually comes around with the correlation of not getting enough rest. We must instill practices in which we are getting the proper amount of rest and ensuring that our bodies are ready for our daily tasks.

Does it seem like when you do not get enough rest and try to make up for it later, your body does not cooperate? You become drowsier and less focused as the day goes on. Simply missing one day of adequate rest and trying to make up for it the next day can throw off your entire system's ability to function. Your body will be more tired than it would have been otherwise, and you may feel a little more worn down as a result. Being tired is not what I mean when I say lazy. Laziness is something completely different, and it comes in a variety of ways.

Laziness is hard to combat because it is so easy to give into. It would be great to lie around all day and have your chores taken care of for you. It would be perfect if someone else dealt with the children when they were spazzing out about this and that. It would be absolute bliss if you could binge-watch all your favorite shows, eat loads of goodies all day, take a warm soothing bath, and have your massage therapist provide a relaxing session every night before bed. Who needs to care about anything else with a life like this? All your bills are paid, and the rest of your work is handled by someone else. This is the type of life of which you have always dreamed. This is what retirement should look like for everyone, right?

Well, not exactly. We have work to do. There is time for leisure and there is time to enjoy the fruits of your labor; but first we must labor. Be wary to not labor for the sake of labor. This too can take an unnecessary toll on your health. However, we are all called to do what the Lord has commanded us to do, as he has made the necessary provisions in our life to fulfill our purpose. We must awaken each day with that purpose, the unique purpose that defines us and the true work that we do—not our nine-to-five, but the work that God has set for us in our effort to satisfy his glory.

The act of being lazy is defined as being averse or disinclined to work, activity, or exertion. It actually takes work or determination to not do any work. Your body naturally wants to be active and move around. Your mind may not want to work (which is ultimately where laziness starts), but your body hurts when you lie around too long. Your extremities become numb, your arteries become clogged with the unhealthy things you eat, and your health slowly starts to deteriorate.

It is unnatural for people to lie around all day, which explains why bedsores form on your body if you are in bed for an extended period. It is completely abnormal for your body to be lazy. It will break down if you do not activate your body parts. The Bible has many discussion points on idle hands as they pertain to not working. In Genesis, God worked for six days and rested on the seventh day. This is the basic principle for our working lives as well.

To place further emphasis on the necessity of working, the following Bible verses can be used as references to understand the impact of what it means to be lazy. Ecclesiastes 10:18 states, "Through sloth the roof sinks in, and through indolence the house leaks." Do not allow your house to fall apart because of idle hands. This phrase applies not only to a home, but can be used to describe churches, your relationship with your significant other, or your work life. Church members must be active in the community in order for the church to live. Your relationships take work, and you must be an active participant in any relationship for it to grow. And your work life is, well . . . work.

If you are lazy about life, things will come apart. It takes you being an active member, concerned about the happenings of your life, for it to not sag. If you are lazy in your relationships and do not work on your connection with your significant other, with your children, with your friends in Christ, and with Christ himself, your relationships will begin to fall apart. Do not allow your life to pass you by. Be an involved participant in your life! Be purposeful in how you activate your life and the role you play in the lives of others. Proverbs 12:24 states, "The hand of the diligent will rule, while the slothful will be put to forced labor." This proverb speaks for itself. We must all be diligent in whatever it is that we do.

In *Animal Farm* by George Orwell, the pigs ruled the farm because they took the time to become better educated and used their intelligence against the other animals. They were able to set the rules of government for the entire farm, creating a have vs. have-not relationship.[1] The premise of rich vs. poor often can be defined by how willing you are to work for something. A lot of times, the rules are stacked against the poor, but success and the ability to overcome life's difficulties requires work. Proverbs 10:4–5 states, "A slack hand causes poverty, but the hand of the diligent makes rich. He who gathers in summer is a prudent son, but he who sleeps in harvest is a son who brings shame." For those of you who love biblical words of prosperity, I do not know if there is a better statement. Hard work brings forth riches. However, riches are not always (or hardly ever) material things when talking about the Bible. Riches for you may not mean what riches means to me. Love may be enough for me to feel like a rich man. Meanwhile, a thriving and loving relationship with God may be more than enough to make you feel like a rich man.

Proverbs 21:25 states, "The desire of the sluggard kills him, for his hands refuse to labor." Do not allow laziness to ruin your life. Get up and get to work. Those messages about laziness are stated like God himself wrote them. Each verse should reverberate within your spirit as you now understand that it is against biblical principles to be a lazy or idle person.

Laziness takes on many forms. America is one of the laziest countries when considering physical activity. But the US is lazy in so many other ways

---

1. Orwell, *Animal Farm*.

that make it detrimental to live here. There is too much at stake for you to be lazy and not take advantage of everything God has to offer. At the same time, there is a balance between working yourself to death and being lazy. Both are extremes that do not meld well with the spiritual composition of who God wants us to be.

SOCIETAL CONSTRUCTS THAT SUPPORT LAZINESS

This world and its entire social construct have evolved or devolved into a place where the idea of being lazy can manifest itself into something more. For example, people abuse and scam systems like Medicaid for their gain. Some people abuse the SNAP program, which used to be known as food stamps. These programs are designed to help people gain access to healthcare and cover their costs, as well as aid in the purchase of food. Without these programs, some people would be facing true hardship and may not be able to eat. Instead of the program benefitting those in need, it is being deceived by people who try to scam the program or rip off recipients of their benefits.

So many people are just looking to get over. The idea of selling drugs because it is easier than working a job or creating your own legalized way to earn a living is a form of laziness. Yes, you may be out there hours on end hustling, but this profession came because of not wanting to explore legitimate ways of earning a living. Yes, there are societal constructs that are built against some people, but many people have found other ways to make a financial impact on their lives and changed their situation. Being a drug dealer does not have to be one of them. Unfortunately, the idea of hustling and being on the streets to earn a quick buck usually ends in tragedy. This is one societal construct that has taken a deadly toll on America. It is completely unnecessary, yet it has a strong foundation within the fabric of our communities. The toll the drug game has taken on our communities is reprehensible. But even the street's involvement under the umbrella of drug usage is lagging when compared to legalize or prescription drug use and its impact on society.

TECHNOLOGY

Another social construct that we all use to better our lives, that may also be hindering us from engaging with one another in a meaningful way, is the constant evolution of technology. We tend to look at technology as a tool that helps us perform tasks better. However, technology has also disrupted what it means to be human. It interrupts our engagements and relationships.

As a follower of technology and someone who enjoys working with new technology, it is a somber reality for me to admit that we are less inclined to connect personally and more inclined to allow depictions of social interactions to be dictated by technology. But the truth is that as much as technology has improved our day-to-day life, it takes away just as much, when we consider what it means to relate to one another. We have a humanistic connection gap in the US. We are constantly missing the uniqueness and similarities of one another and discounting the importance of every person. Therefore, we tend to dismiss the value of our neighbor's life.

SOCIAL MEDIA

I can recall conversations where people have stated they did not have time to meet with someone in person; however, they may spend hours perusing different social media platforms. Many people have hundreds of friends on the various social media platforms, yet so many of these connections are empty. I have over 500 friends on Facebook, and I was a late adopter of the platform. However, many of these friends with whom I have connected are just random people. I do not have a true relationship with many of them. And the idea of following each other on a social network limits the inclination to make human contact.

We sit next to each other and neglect to speak or say hi. We would rather put our heads down looking at a device and be entertained. We are missing the opportunity to connect with each other. This missed connection may later lead to us dismissing each other. There is value beyond a digital connection.

Social media offers us the platform to be lazy and not engage in real relationships. People do not have time to date another human being before dating them online first. Acclaimed rap artist J. Cole said in his song "She's Mine Pt. 2," "We don't love, we just liking sh** here."[2] He is right. This is the new way we interact with each other. There is no real attachment to one another. This is the epitome of reading a book by its cover, when the cover and the story may be based on a false perception. We must be more proactive in the relationships we establish. Technology should not replace human contact or human relationships. It should serve only to enhance them. These relationships we are neglecting are the ones on which God wants us to work and in which he wants us to invest our time.

2. Cole, "She's Mine Pt. 2."

CYBERBULLYING

With access to more technology comes an unfortunate negative element for our children in the form of cyberbullying. Bullying Statistics was created to discuss the growing epidemic of bullying and cyberbullying, stating, "Suicide is the third leading cause of death among young people, resulting in 4,400 deaths per year."[3] Studies performed by Yale suggest "victims of bullies are between two to nine times more likely to commit suicide at some point in their teenage years."[4]

These rates are alarming, and technology creates the playing field where such behavior can transpire without fear of repercussion. Cyberbullies can hide behind their online identities while causing a tremendous amount of pain within the lives of others. We cannot allow technology to reduce the role of being human toward one another through relationships. Perhaps, if a bully would take the time to know the person he is bullying, he may come to find that they have a lot in common. The connection to one another is important here. However, the laziness of not taking the time to know someone creates a barrier between two people instead of bridging the gap. Many times, the shelter of technology appears to embolden the bullying behavior.

Our children are suffering right in front of us while we give them access to technology without fully understanding or exploring what is happening when we are not watching. We are also unsure of how we can intervene as parents. The social construct of technology, bullying, and finding a way to lessen its impact is being addressed by several organizations, yet it remains a prevalent problem within society. If we are going to move in the direction of allowing social media and technology to play a role in our lives and the lives of our children, we must educate our children through active dialogue. They should feel comfortable coming to us for support if they feel bullied or threatened.

They should feel supported by a safe and loving relationship with their parents. We must let our children know they do not have to face bullying alone. They must understand that we are there to nurture them no matter what they may be going through. If your child is the perpetrator, please connect with him or her before these actions get out of hand and cause irreparable damage. Many times, children who are bullies come from a home with a loved one who may also be a bully. This is an unfortunate circle of poor behavior choices, but it is one where the parents must remain involved

---

3. Bullying Statistics, "Bullying and Suicide."
4. CDC, "Relationship between Bullying and Suicide."

to address their bullying antics in the home, as well as helping their child solve their disgruntled issues. Cyberbullying masks the opportunity for intervention, but if we raise our children to love one another, as God loves us, we create an opportunity for togetherness.

TECHNOLOGY AND ELECTIONS

Technology is also a tool that is becoming a pivotal mechanism for communication for our elected officials. Whether we agree on the role of technology and the way we interact with elected representatives, we should recognize the power it wields as an influential component of elections. President Obama used several platforms to communicate with the American populace, drumming up an audience and striking a connection with America's youth. By the same token, Russian influence has been blamed for the outcome of the 2016 presidential election.

These are some of the roles in which we allow technology to evolve and influence our lives. We appreciate the modernization of life due to technology. However, we must remain in touch with one another beyond the scope of technological enhancements, since we have yet to fully understand or appreciate each other. Technology is essential to our daily living; however, we need to know how to engage with one another outside the use of technology and not foster a behavior of laziness where it deteriorates our need for human relations, thus enabling everyone to become strangers, even in politics. Technology can be used as a rallying cry, as we later found out, to misinform people about the governance of this country. We cannot lazily rely on technology to tell us of what actually matters; God's word does that.

CONVENIENCE

We are living in a society driven by convenience. This time in history is often referred to as the microwave generation, where the convenience of everything allows you to be lazy in your choices about life. This is especially true when it comes to eating. Fast-food restaurants and processed foods obtained through your local grocery store offer convenience at low prices to encourage you to consider them as an option instead of eating meals prepared at home or making healthier food choices. These companies make money on the idea of providing you with quick meals, but at what cost to your health? It is not a bold statement that fried fast food is terrible for you. Even restaurants that tout healthier alternatives often add ingredients that make those healthy options just as unhealthy as a burger and fries.

In the US, food choices are unbelievably unhealthy. Internationally, these same fast-food restaurants provide better food options for their consumers. The menus are completely different internationally than what citizens in the US receive. It is like restaurants dump their garbage on Americans and we sift through it, trying to find the greasiest thing to buy. We must pay attention and not allow convenience to corrupt our health. These fast-food companies do not care about you or your health. The only time they offer a healthier option is when they are pressured to do so by some federal mandate, trends, or, more importantly, dollars. We are left to our own devices, trying to find the best food items to eat that will not cause our bodies harm. And if you live in a poor neighborhood, good luck trying to find something that has not been manufactured or is not unhealthy for you to consume.

Wealthier neighborhoods have options like MOMs or Whole Foods that offer better choices of food options for their consumers. The poorer you are, the fewer options you have when selecting grocers or restaurant options for you and your family. Even when you purchase healthier foods in a fast-food restaurant, they tend to cost more than the unhealthier options. The price of a salad is typically more than the price of a burger and fries at most restaurants. Therefore, if you have minimal income or if you are living paycheck to paycheck, buying the cheaper alternative food is sometimes all you can afford.

McDonald's previously admitted to using genetically modified organisms (GMO) in some dishes. GMOs are completely banned in Russia and France, yet they are available in the US. Keep in mind that Russia is reportedly a country whose leadership has not shied away from poisoning its citizens for political reasons, yet they banned GMOs.

According to Jeffrey Smith, journalist for Responsibletechnology.org, GMOs' impact in animal studies shows organ damage, gastrointestinal and immune system disorders, accelerated aging, and infertility that can occur when using GMO products.[5] Yet, McDonald's has served foods containing GMOs to people for years, and they are not the only restaurant. The salads you receive from these restaurants are also filled with loads of fat content and calories. The worst culprit of convenience eating is pizza. There are enough calories in some pizza options to cover your recommended calorie intake for a day and a half. Just as an aside, anytime there is grease dripping from the food packaging, you should probably think twice about eating that food. Many people indulge in poor food choices every so often; however, your body begins to break down when all you consume are these unhealthy

---

5. Smith, "Ten Reasons to Avoid GMOs."

food choices. Let us take care of our bodies like God asks of us. It does not matter what marketing campaign we see, or how we were raised, or our access to convenient food options: the choice is ours to improve our health.

MAKING A CHANGE

We cannot be lazy with our food choices or our health. First Corinthians 10:31 says, "So whether you eat or drink, or whatever you do, do all to the glory of God." God does not judge us for the foods we eat. However, our bodies are his temple, and we should take care to preserve all that God has given us. We should take the necessary steps to cook more often and limit the unhealthy items we put in our bodies like oils and butter. We must take our health into our hands, because these companies are not going to do it for us. The first step to addressing our health is eating well. We must move toward a mentality that is focused on improving our eating habits and seeking healthier alternatives instead of corroding our arteries.

Being passive with our eating habits, as well as creating an overall state of laziness, plagues our nation and provides an alarmingly unhealthy diagnosis for America's future. Below are obesity and overweight data from a study performed by the CDC reviewing adults ages twenty and older:

- More than two-thirds (68.8 percent) of adults are overweight or obese.
- Almost three in four men (74 percent) are overweight or obese.
- The prevalence of obesity is similar for both men and women (about 36 percent).[6]

OBESITY AND DEATH

Frankly speaking, we should take our health seriously. Some of our health issues are genetically inclined, but many of the challenges we face can be addressed by making better decisions. Your heart and your overall health cannot wait any longer for you to change your mind regarding eating habits.

When two-thirds of America's population is overweight, we must have our priorities wrong. We are not just obese; we are dying because of it. I am a believer that the health system is flawed, and our country's BMI index is used to make you feel bad about your weight. However, there are some facts that we cannot ignore.

6. CDC, "National Health and Nutrition Examination Survey."

Dr. Joseph Mercola wrote an article on his website highlighting that "One in five people in America die due to obesity."[7] Stress, obesity, and heart disease are real American issues. According to the National Institutes of Health, "Obesity and overweight together are the second leading cause of preventable death with an estimated 300,000 deaths per year due to the obesity epidemic."[8]

One factor that contributes to the high level of obesity is the incredible amount of television we watch per day. What are we doing while watching TV? We are primarily sitting around and possibly eating something processed. When you put these factors together, it is a recipe for continued American obesity. "Children between the ages of two and eleven watched over twenty-four hours of television a week,"[9] according to Nielsen Media Ratings Company. This study did not factor in how much a role our addiction to technology plays in us just sitting around. So much of how we live and the things that contribute to us being lazy can be easily controlled. We should be disciplined enough to stand up for our health. We must take the necessary steps to improve our lives.

BE USEFUL BEYOND LAZY

We cannot afford to allow our lives to be ruined by laziness. God cannot use a lazy person to forward his plans. I have seen the disparities related to how laziness can affect people. For example, I have a cousin, as of this writing, who is sixty-seven years old and another relative in his late fifties. On a trip to South Carolina, I met with the sixty-seven-year-old cousin as he just left his animals and his farming activities. The younger relative remarked to the older relative that he was one tough S.O.B. since he is active and always moving. The younger relative is not as active and is not as mobile. He does not work a farm or maintain high levels of activity. Both are men, live in the same area, and have a similar socioeconomic status. They also have achieved similar educational attainment. However, the major difference between the two, other than age, is one ensures he is active and says, "As long as God keeps me here, I will remain active." He states, "That is the best way to stay alive."

He also mentioned that he has a ninety-two-year-old friend who is just as active and refuses to stop moving. Both the ninety-two-year-old friend and the sixty-seven-year-old cousin believe that if they stop being active,

---

7. Mercola, "One in Five American Deaths."

8. National Institute of Diabetes and Digestive and Kidney Diseases, "Overweight and Obesity Statistics."

9. Nielsen Company, "Kids' Audience Behavior."

they will die. That may be a bit drastic, but both men are relatively healthy and highly active. The relative in his late fifties, however, is not as healthy or active. He has also been afflicted with several ailments and health issues.

I am not saying that the activity level is the only reason there are discrepancies in their health statuses. However, I believe it plays a part. There are other issues like genetics or sometimes the cards are just not in your favor. Knowing these two individuals, I think activity or the lack thereof contributes to their health gap. Perhaps it is just a mindset and belief that God will take care of you if you keep diligent hands is the prevailing reason their health indicators are so far apart.

ACTIVE AND FIT AND ENGAGE LIFE AT ANY AGE

There are many instances where older people state that being active keeps them healthy. I admire Ernestine Shepard, a seventy-nine-year-old fitness guru living in Maryland. Michelle Nati wrote an article covering ten women who looked decades younger.[10] Nati wrote that Ms. Shepard started working out later in life around her mid-fifties after she was displeased by how she looked. Many people can relate to feeling like Ms. Shepard. The article also states, "Ernestine was named World's Oldest Performing Female Bodybuilder by the Guinness Book of World Records in 2010." These are actually #goals toward which to aspire. A lot of older people do not want to stop working because they believe their health will begin to fail, so they develop a habit of remaining active.

I admire these people for their resiliency and their efforts to maintain an active life. Just as these people have made a change in their lives, we must also take time to make the necessary adjustments in our lives. We must discover the next steps in our destiny to live on purpose. We cannot let the idea of being lazy come to fruition, no matter how convenient unhealthy options may be. Make it your life's work to stay active and remain that way, so God can use you the way he wants to. He cannot use us if we are sitting down and not actively pursuing him. God cannot use us if we are lazy about life and lazy about him. We must remain diligent and never be content with a lifestyle that is not the best for us. God does not want that for us. Let us get to know each other better. Do not allow technology, convenience, or simply an unwillingness to engage with life and with each other to limit who we were meant to be in the eyes of God.

---

10. Nati, "Ten Older Women."

Challenge 7

Overindulging (Sex, Drugs, and Alcohol)

Everything in Moderation Is More Than Just a Saying

Everything in moderation, too much of anything can be a bad thing, and just say no are statements used to describe self-control when discussing the idea of overindulgence. These are statements you have probably heard at some point in your life. These are also statements that you can apply to America's infatuation with sex, drugs, and alcohol. When used too much, any of these vices tends to take control of your body's normal functioning and become addictions. Often, the users are unable to stop the cravings of these vices without seeking professional help.

Sex, drugs, and alcohol are all addictions stemming directly from the concept of overindulgence. Think about the first time you had sex, had a drink, or tried some drugs (marijuana, molly, ecstasy, or some other variety of drugs). Were you pressured by your peers? Did you see your parents doing it? Was it something you heard in a song and thought it would be cool to try? Did you see people doing it on TV and thought you should give it a try too? Most of our engagements in risky behaviors start because someone told us to do it. Perhaps we saw someone else participating in one of these activities and thought we could do it as well. We usually believe our participation in these activities will not have any significant consequences on our lives or the lives of our loved ones.

Unfortunately, there may be serious penalties for our actions. *U.S. News* journalist Lloyd Sederer references a study by Columbia University which finds that forty million Americans ages twelve and over meet the clinical criteria for addiction involving nicotine, alcohol, or other drugs.[1] That is more Americans than those with heart disease, diabetes, or cancer. Additionally, Sederer notes that an estimated eighty million people in this country are "risky substance users," meaning that, while not addicted, they "use tobacco, alcohol and other drugs in ways that threaten public health and safety." Do you or anyone you know fall into any of these categories?

MY EXPOSURE TO OVERINDULGENCE

While I have never been addicted to alcohol, sex, or drugs, I have been acquainted with people who struggled with both alcohol and drugs. As of this writing, I have been inebriated twice in my life, and I am not a fan of how it made me feel. I did not like losing control of my body or my words due to overindulgence in a substance like alcohol. And I was informed that I tend to talk a great deal when I drink too much. I am what they call a lightweight when it comes to drinking. Based on my own experience, I am an advocate for drinking in moderation. I have never smoked weed or tried any harder drugs, primarily because of a promise I made to my three-year-old sister. I told her I would never do drugs or become an alcoholic. So, I plan to remain true to my words.

However, I have witnessed family members who struggled mightily with alcoholism. Their entire lives were turned upside down. They were helpless to do anything about their downward spiral, because alcohol was altering their capacity to make appropriate decisions. Their family left them and some even lost their homes, partly due to their alcohol addiction. Being able to have a firsthand account of how alcohol ruined the lives of these family members taught me to not subject myself to this lifestyle.

Overindulging in other vices like smoking plagued people I knew as well. My grandmother used to smoke cigarettes every day. Of course, she never sought help or cared to call it an addiction, but she would go through a pack of Kool cigarettes in two days. She would send my cousins and me to the neighborhood store to purchase cigarettes when we were kids (which was illegal) and we would buy her some Kools. We would ride our bikes back to the house and sometimes light them for her on the stovetop. This

---

1. Sederer, "Blind Eye to Addiction."

was as close as I have ever been to smoking a cigarette. I thought the taste was so bad that I had no problem saying I was never going to become a smoker. However, my distaste for cigarettes never caused my grandmother's affection toward them to waver. Although her addiction to cigarettes was not the ultimate cause of her death at the age of sixty-five, I am sure they did not help her health matters either.

I also worked with a woman in her forties who struggled with smoking. She had unexplainable ailments and a raspy voice, which I thought could be attributed to her addiction. She understood that smoking was something she needed to stop but stated that she couldn't shake the habit. We had a discussion one time regarding the constant pain she was experiencing in her back, and she could not figure out why. The doctors could not help her understand what was causing her this pain either, but they all kept saying the same thing: lose weight and stop smoking. She tried to stop smoking but to no avail. Each day at the office, she would take five or six breaks to go and smoke a cigarette. It was like the relationship with her cigarettes was a terrible affair. She could not break up with the cigarettes without going right back later, although she knew the cigarettes were abusing her. She later said to me during one of our watercooler conversations, "Why are all of the things you like doing bad for you?" She said, "You can't drink, smoke, have sex, or eat a burger."

I thought about this conversation and laughed to myself shortly afterward. These are vices that are meant to please your flesh, not your spirit. Therefore, they feel good to your flesh, but your flesh is a foolish thing. Your spirit needs something more.

I have also had relationships with people who have sold and used drugs. Some of these people were family members, and others were individuals with whom I went to school with or whom I met in passing. It does not matter what side of the drug spectrum people are on; the result can lead to premature death. I have lost many childhood friends to drug-related situations, and I can say I consider myself lucky to have avoided that lifestyle from either side of the spectrum.

I have heard personal accounts where people have done terrible things for drugs such as stealing, having sex with random people, or just being lost in the world. Of the people I have met with various addictions, drugs are seemingly the most painful to watch. These people literally cannot help themselves. Being an addict typically takes a toll on everyone involved.

With all of America's freedoms, we have yet to figure out how to establish our freedom of saying no to the overindulgence of vices that are killing us. We seek them out as a form of escape; all the while, we become more of a prisoner than we ever were.

SEX

The topic of sex is not only related to those who have addictions but more to the idea of unprotected sex and premarital relationships. If you are married and in a faithful relationship, have as much sex as you like. Pastor Jeffrey A. Johnson Sr., the senior pastor of Eastern Star Church in Indianapolis, wrote in his book *Song of Solomon* how people are supposed to love and be intimate with a significant other as a married couple.[2] In his book, he provides details regarding God's purpose for intimacy. In several of Pastor Johnson's sermons, he quotes Hebrews 13:4, stating that "in the marriage bedroom, everything is undefiled."[3] To offer you more context regarding why having sex while married is the ultimate act of intimacy, please read 1 Corinthians 7:1–5 thoroughly.

First Corinthians gives us a principle or two regarding the proper sexual relationship within marriage. Each person should regard his or her body as belonging to his or her mate and not under one's own total control to do with it whatever one pleases. Sex should be refrained from only by agreement for the purpose of fasting and prayer, after which time the couple should come together sexually, so that they are not tempted to fulfill their needs elsewhere. Love and sex know no bounds when you are married.

This is the way we are supposed to practice healthy sexual relationships. Feel free to take your husband or wife to limitless displays of affection for one another. That is the way God intended sex to be within the boundaries of marriage. We should not explore sex outside of the boundaries of marriage, especially if you are married. Your partner should be willing to give all of himself or herself to you, and you should be willing to do the same.

ME AND SEX

Sex becomes a problem when marriage is not involved, and we indulge in premarital fornication or adultery. I am not a saint when it comes to premarital sex. I engaged in premarital sex, believing it was something I wanted to be good at by the time I was married. Besides, I knew others were doing it, so my interest was piqued as well. I was considered a late bloomer to my friends—and to my mother, for that matter.

My high school football teammates would joke about my virginity like it was something of which I should feel ashamed instead of something that would make God proud. Like a kid that could not withstand peer pressure,

---

2. J. Johnson, *Song of Solomon*.
3. See BibleStudy.org, "What Is Defiling."

I wanted to lose my virginity to escape the idea of having to worry about it anymore.

As a young boy, you want to be a part of the in-crowd and not have sex be an issue within your life. It is perfectly natural to feel as if you need to fit in with everyone else. But little did I know that God seeks out those who are outcasts or those who are not with the in-crowd. Those people who have been pushed aside are the people God wants to pick up to do his will. But being as fallible as I am, I fell into my lustful desires, like so many others. However, I wanted my first experience to be with someone I cared about, not just some available girl. I was deathly afraid of having children out of wedlock and would not dare have sex with someone I could not foresee potentially having a child with at some point.

In any case, I was a complete and utter simpleton for being pressured into having sex. You should not make that decision until you are ready, preferably when you are married. I am not sure if losing my virginity in high school—and a few times afterward—helped at all, but my marital sex life is absolute bliss. As of this writing, to quote the Bible, we have been knowing each other for over twelve years as a couple, and we continuously reach new levels of showing each other what love is. When your significant other is truly the one God has for you, sex is worth the wait.

PREMARITAL SEX AND ITS IMPACT

Based on the way of the world today, premarital sex is not all it is cracked up to be. Many times, I have heard women say they wished they had waited or selected another partner. Premarital sex has consequences, and sometimes these consequences—children out of wedlock or an STD—may stick around for your lifetime.

According to the American Sexual Health Association (ASHA), "more than half of all people will have an STD/STI at some point in their lifetime."[4] This statistic speaks to how reckless we are when engaging in acts of intercourse while neglecting their negative consequences. STDs have been spreading like the black plague. The effects of premarital sex and adultery are running rampant through our communities, and we are paying for our indiscretions. I do not believe we can stop premarital sex within our society, but I am hopeful we can stop the rise of STDs and STIs.

As I mentioned, I have two young girls, and the thought of them having sex drives me insane. I completely comprehend that it may be inevitable, but it is just that I changed their stinky bottoms, and, like most involved

4. American Sexual Health Association, "STDs: A to Z."

parents, I believe they will be my precious little daughters forever. However, understanding how much of a role sex plays within our society, it is scary to accept that it is a high probability that one of my daughters may contract an STD at some point in her life.

The Centers for Disease Control and Infection report that there are "19.7 million new STIs every year in the U.S."[5] STIs and STDs are devastating epidemics. Thankfully, not all STDs and STIs are fatal.

The staggering numbers below show how rapidly STDs are spreading within our communities. We must practice safety within our sexual encounters by either waiting or wearing protection. We can try practicing abstinence as well.

I know I mentioned that stopping premarital sex may be difficult to do, but the consequences of experimenting with poor sexual practices are life-threatening. Of the nearly twenty million new STIs that occur every year, half of those are among young people ages fifteen to twenty-four.[6] These statistics show how the devastation is impacting our youth. Below are some key stats that were published by the ASHA supporting my theory on how premarital sex negatively impacts our lives within the US.

- Each year, one in four teens contracts an STD/STI.
- One in two sexually active persons will contract an STD/STI by age twenty-five.
- It is estimated that as many as one in five Americans have genital herpes, yet up to 90 percent of those with herpes are unaware they have it.
- Over fourteen million people acquire HPV each year, and by age fifty, at least 80 percent of women will have acquired genital HPV infection.[7]

In addition to the incredible rate at which we are contracting STDs in America, the CDC states that more than 1300 cases of congenital syphilis were reported in 2018, resulting in severe health complications and deaths among newborns.[8] The unsatiated sexual appetite in this country is not allowing newborns the opportunity to live.

It is also estimated that undiagnosed STDs cause infertility in more than 20,000 women each year.[9] These stats indicate that we are having too much unprotected sex in this country. It is astounding that, by the age of

5. CDC, "Sexually Transmitted Disease Surveillance."
6. CDC, "Sexually Transmitted Disease Surveillance."
7. American Sexual Health Association, "STDs: A to Z."
8. World Health Organization, "WHO Publishes New Estimates."
9. CDC, "Sexually Transmitted Disease Surveillance."

twenty-five, most of us will have had some sort of STD/STI. Many people use the excuse of not practicing safe sex by saying they do not like how a condom feels. But if you are going to participate in premarital sex, I hope these stats encourage you to think twice about using a condom before you act. If you are married and are committing adultery—which God loathes—please protect your significant other. Tell him or her as soon as possible so he or she can be protected from your poor decisions. Women are often caught off guard by their husbands' indiscretions. We must protect each other for a better future.

SEX: THE BIBLE AND THE PARENTS' IMPACT

God despises adultery so much that he made it a commandment. However, based on our actions, it appears we no longer care about the words of guidance from the Bible, since 15 to 20 percent of married couples cheat. The words within 1 Corinthians 6:18 are clear: flee from sexual immorality. There are a lot of sins that a person can commit outside the body, but the sexually immoral person sins against his own body. Self-control is pivotal; otherwise, it would not take long for half of everyone to change the statistic that 80 percent of everyone will be afflicted by an STD.

I mentioned the high number of single mothers in this country, which is mainly due to unprotected premarital sex. But I did not mention how many children died because of their parents' decision and the ending result being some STD or STI. Our newborns are not able to protect themselves from our actions. If we think our sex lives are not affecting others, consider the following statistics from the World Health Organization, which state that syphilis in pregnancy leads to approximately 305,000 fetal and neonatal deaths every year and leaves 215,000 infants at increased risk of dying from prematurity, low-birthweight, or congenital disease.[10]

We are killing our children before they have a chance to breathe due to our promiscuous behaviors. If the listed reasons are not enough to encourage us to think of our future and how sex plays a role within the construct of America, I am not sure what else can stimulate this nation to act for the sake of its continuation. The thought of the US becoming so overwhelmed with STDs that it becomes crippled may seem far-fetched and outlandish. However, HPV is a leading cause of cervical cancer, impacting almost 80 percent of all women by the age of fifty.[11] Although HPV was discovered in the nineteenth century, we are still learning more about this disease that is

10. World Health Organization, "WHO Publishes New Estimates."
11. Braaten and Laufer, "Human Papillomavirus (HPV)."

changing the lives of women every day. Sodom and Gomorrah paid a price for their sexual promiscuity; we should be more careful.

Sex is an amazing experience when you follow the guidelines God has already outlined for intimacy. All you need to know is Proverbs 5:18-19, which states, "Let your fountain be blessed, and rejoice in the wife of your youth, a lovely deer, a graceful doe. Let her breasts fill you at all times with delight; be intoxicated always in her love." Take this course of action and follow God's path. The sex we have should always be within the confines of God's guidance. God is the reason. He is intimacy. The things we do outside of God's directions—even something that can be as pleasurable as sex—always lead to destruction.

DRUGS

America's drug habit is no surprise to anyone, and the opioid epidemic has acted as a catalyst for making this a pivotal issue. Americans experiment with more drugs than do the people of any other country, and our children are the guinea pigs for what is new on the streets. The US had the war on drugs, which tried to tackle the epidemic of drugs, but it was more like a socioeconomically charged program that disproportionally targeted minorities.

The consumption of drugs is seemingly at an all-time high. Many people are experimenting with new drugs or finding new ways to blend drugs for a more potent high. Although there have been programs like Drug Abuse Resistance Education (DARE) placed in public schools to discourage children from trying drugs, there has been a steady increase in deaths by drug overdoses since 2000. These deaths are not only caused by drugs like heroin and crack. These deaths are also caused by opioids and other over-the-counter drugs. I think it is a mistake to call out opioids as the problem and not address the concept of addiction or identify the true source behind the disease of addictive behaviors. If opioids were not the culprit, Americans would find another unfortunate avenue to self-medicate.

The National Institute on Drug Abuse (NIDA) states, "In 2013 an estimated 24.6 million Americans aged twelve or older—9.4 percent of the population—had used an illicit drug in the past."[12] This number was up from 8.3 percent in 2002. The report also stated the increase mostly reflects a recent rise in the use of marijuana, the most commonly used illicit drug. A staggering 9.4 percent of the country has used an illicit drug in any month.

12. National Institute on Drug Abuse, "Trends and Statistics."

These numbers will likely increase with twenty-five states and Washington DC recently approving the use of medical marijuana.

I liken the idea of trying drugs to the way companies target new customers. Many companies tend to take what I call the McDonald's approach to marketing and growing their business. These companies start targeting children at young ages with marketing strategies or products like a Happy Meal to entice children or teens. The goal is to attract these young consumers while they are impressionable and then hook them for life. This marketing strategy goes a long way in increasing the company's customer lifetime value. The customer lifetime value is another way to say how much money a company can expect to make on a customer throughout that person's engagement with the company (or their lifetime as a customer).

The drug industry operates similarly. Most people begin experimenting with drugs when they are teenagers. Unfortunately, these experiments tend to grow into long-lasting relationships. A teenager's first encounter with drugs is typically encouraged by friends. As the character Craig Jones, portrayed by Ice Cube in the 1995 movie *Friday*, says, "Peer pressure is a mother******."[13] The introduction to drugs normally starts with some form of peer pressure.

However, anyone who encourages someone to do drugs or stands by while another person pushes a needle filled with poison into their bloodstream is not a friend. That person does not care about the user's well-being. That person does not care if the user lives to see tomorrow, because that person is too busy living for the moment as well. As I discussed during the relationship section, you must be aware of whom you choose to classify as a friend. Everyone who laughs in your presence is not necessarily laughing with you; that person may be laughing at you. This is similar to the trials of Job.

Job thought he had friends until he was going through his terrible ailments. He soon found out that his friends offered no support. Instead, they ridiculed him and blamed him for his situation, although it was God allowing Satan to torture Job, since he was considered a faithful servant. Job called the people scorning him "miserable friends." If a friend can watch you kill yourself or destroy your life, then you too have miserable friends. They are worse than Job's friends. His friends only blamed him for his situation. However, those so-called friends who would watch another friend attempt suicide or take chances with his or her life are surely not friends. Each time someone takes a hit of cocaine or heroin or indulges in excessive opioid use or any other similar drug, there is an inherent flirtation with death.

13. Gray, dir., *Friday*.

DRUG ABUSE BY THE NUMBERS

The NIDA report discusses how fast people are being introduced to illicit drugs, stating there were just over 2.8 million new users of illicit drugs in 2013 or about 7,800 new users per day. Over half (54.1 percent) were under eighteen years of age.[14] Marijuana is typically the drug of choice by most teens, which is why it is known as the gateway drug.

I have never smoked marijuana of any kind or flavor; therefore, I cannot speak personally to its effects on a person's body. But I know many people who have smoked marijuana or tried some variation. Some of them have graduated to stronger drugs and have completely spiraled out of control. On the other hand, I know people who use only marijuana and live productive lives.

Some people smoke marijuana or other drugs and may be able to control their indulgence. But older people are also beginning to experiment with drugs more now than at any point in history. Over seventeen percent of adults between the ages of fifty and sixty-four used drugs in 2013.[15]

These stats explain that we have a problem with drugs that cannot be overstated. The death toll from drug overdoses is too much to bear. Sederer reports that over 38,000 people died of drug overdoses in the US in 2010, greater than the deaths attributed to motor vehicle accidents, homicides, and suicides. Overdose deaths from opioids (narcotic pills like Oxycontin, Percodan, and Methadone, as well as heroin) have become the fastest-growing drug problem throughout the US, and not just in large urban settings.[16] Many people believe the opioid epidemic was an issue well before it became publicized. However, when the addiction became known outside urban areas, the nation began to pay attention. According to International Overdose Awareness Day, "America averaged 43,982 deaths per year, which is an average of 120 deaths per day that is related to drugs."[17] As of this writing, 2014 was the highest total ever for people who died from drug overdoses. How frightening is this number?

This problem was concealed from the masses until several high-profile celebrities died due to prescription overdose or opioid use. Most recently, the world lost Prince to the powerful drug. In addition to Prince, Philip Seymour Hoffman, Glee actor Cory Monteith, Heath Ledger, Chris Farley, Michael Jackson, Elvis Presley, and Anna Nicole Smith are a few well-known

---

14. National Institute on Drug Abuse, "Trends and Statistics."
15. National Institute on Drug Abuse, "Trends and Statistics."
16. Sederer, "Blind Eye to Addiction."
17. International Overdose Awareness Day, "Facts and Stats."

people who have died due to drug overdose.[18] But there are thousands of people suffering the same fate

The Bible does not specifically discuss drugs, because these are items created by man. God speaks directly for and to everything he created, including you. And although the Bible does not specifically say to not use drugs, it does discuss your body directly. You are to cherish your body, because it is God's temple. You are not to worship or be influenced by earthly things, and drugs are derived from the earth.

If you are addicted to drugs, you are not in control of yourself or your actions. You are being influenced by something that is not of God, which often leads to destruction. Christians are commanded to present their bodies to God as instruments of righteousness, according to Romans 6:13. Even if you are not a Christian, your body is still a temple that you should protect. There is no way you can give yourself to God and to drugs. One will not allow the other to thrive. You must give up drugs for the sake of your children, for the sake of your future, and for the fear of God.

As I stated, I have been under the influence of alcohol twice. I did not like the way it made me feel, and I did not like that I was not in control of my body or my actions. I could tell I was off, but there was not much I could do at that point. I knew that I was not wholly in charge of my body. We are to bring our bodies under control and not be controlled by our bodily appetites, says 1 Corinthians 9:24-27.

Drugs speak to our bodily appetites. They are chemical compounds created to provide the flesh with a feeling unlike that made by God. These feelings are unwarranted by the Father, which is why people seemingly lose all sense of being when they are under the influence. Drugs control your body. Therefore, people can take advantage of you when you are under the influence. You only get one chance at this life. Do not misuse it by allowing something that is not of you to make you do things you would not normally do. Give God the wheel to control your life, and run away from things that are not like him. Overindulgence of drugs of all kinds is not like him.

ALCOHOL

Alcohol use has been on decline in recent years; however, wine consumption in comparison to other types of alcohol has increased. I guess our taste buds are into the finer things in life. We are indulging in a little more of a refined taste, as beer seems to not be the alcoholic beverage of choice any longer. In either case, America still has a bit of a drinking problem.

18. LaMotte, "Celebrities Who Died."

The National Council on Alcoholism and Drug Dependence states, "Alcohol is the most commonly used addictive substance in the United States. Over 17.6 million people, or one in every twelve adults, suffer from alcohol abuse or dependence, along with several million more who engage in risky, binge drinking patterns."[19] No one is immune from the lure and seemingly pleasurable guise of alcohol, since pastors and leaders of faith have fallen victim to overindulgence in this addictive behavior.

My family has had its bouts with alcoholism. I have two close relatives who lost everything due to their addiction to alcohol. It is a continuous cycle that haunts the abusers and seems as if it cannot be broken. Even as the consumers of alcohol are watching their lives fall apart (and are completely aware that nothing is going right within their lives), they are typically defenseless and cannot stop it. It is sad to witness someone struggle with alcoholism, especially if it is a loved one and you do not have the means to intervene or help.

Usually, the decision to fight alcoholism must be made by the person who is struggling with the addiction. I remember engaging in a conversation with one of my relatives who was suffering from alcoholism. He lamented to me after his family left, saying, "You don't miss your water until your well runs dry," quoting a classic song written by William Bell. I will always remember those words, as they were a part of the most profound conversation that we have ever had.

Sometimes you watch people wake up in the morning, and the first thing they do is grab an alcoholic beverage to drink. Then they finish their day with more drinks, until they are completely inebriated. It is heartbreaking to see the drastic difference in their personalities when they are intoxicated versus when they have good days. It becomes a little scary, especially to younger children, when the intoxicated days outweigh the sober days. Children who watch family members partake in this behavior are at a higher risk of becoming alcoholics or participating in these types of activities as well. This holds true for my relative, as his son struggled with his own issues as well. People who are under the influence obtain what is deemed liquid courage and say or do things they would not normally do under a sober frame of mind. These actions often lead to poor judgments.

Sometimes, the intoxicated person may lash out or do something reckless like driving while being under the influence. My relatives have done ludicrous things while being under the influence, but I am grateful that both are still alive—although their battle with alcoholism is not over. We can count it as a blessing that God is not done with them yet. I guess there

---

19. National Council on Alcoholism and Drug Dependence, "Facts about Alcohol."

THE PERILS OF ALCOHOL

The National Institute on Alcohol Abuse and Alcoholism (NIAAA) states, "Nearly 88,000 people die from alcohol-related causes annually, making alcohol the fourth leading preventable cause of death in the United States."[20] However, just because something is preventable does not mean that we will take the initiative to limit the devastation. The NIAAA found that in 2014, alcohol-impaired driving fatalities accounted for 9,967 deaths (31 percent of overall driving fatalities). The issue with alcoholism is not only a US issue. Globally, alcohol-related burdens contributed to over 3.3 million deaths or 5.9 percent of all global deaths in 2012, the NIAAA reports. Alcoholism is not always an individual vice. It usually takes a toll on other people. Oftentimes your loved ones are left to pick up the pieces.

For example, a father in Georgia was believed to have been drinking on August 4, 2016. Due to his seemingly drunken state, he accidentally left his fifteen-month-old twins in a hot car that day.[21] The twins did not survive the sweltering heat of the car, although the father later tried to revive them. Now, this young family is torn apart as the father faces involuntary manslaughter charges in the deaths of his beloved little girls. Accidents like this happen all the time, but with the additional influence of alcohol, as in this case, we are made to forget the most precious things in our lives.

We deal with conditions like cancer that can show up at any time just because we are alive, but when we have to contend with preventable conditions like alcoholism, we are creating a mountain that may be too hard to climb. Alcoholism contributes to over two hundred diseases and injury-related health conditions, like liver cirrhosis and alcohol dependence.[22]

Alcohol, like most addictions, significantly impacts our children. NIAAA's study shows that, globally, "alcohol misuse is the fifth leading risk factor for premature death and disability; among people between the ages of fifteen and forty-nine, it is the first. In the age group twenty to thirty-nine years, approximately 25 percent of the total deaths are alcohol-attributable."[23] The CDC adds that "of the 1,070 traffic deaths among children ages zero to

---

20. NIAAA, "Alcohol Facts and Statistics."
21. Fieldstadt, "Georgia Dad Charged."
22. NIAAA, "Alcohol Facts and Statistics."
23. NIAAA, "Alcohol Facts and Statistics."

fourteen in 2014, 19 percent involved an alcohol-impaired driver."[24] This is a tragic and unfortunate lost of life that could have been avoided.

While the magnitude of these numbers may be difficult to comprehend, think of how many lives can be saved just by basic alcohol education. As a country, we should take more responsibility for what we put into our bodies and the effects of overindulgence. The adverse effects are not always deadly, but they are life-changing nonetheless.

ALCOHOL AND SCHOOL

When we factor in college and the role alcohol plays in the lives of college students, the culmination of incidents that are alcohol-related is staggering. NIAAA researchers estimate the following happens on college campuses each year:

- 1,696,000 students between the ages of eighteen and twenty-four are assaulted by another student who has been drinking.
- Roughly twenty percent of college students meet the criteria for an alcohol use disorder (AUD).[25]

Parents send their children away to college each year, and they understand their babies will certainly have changed before they return home. However, parents do not want that change to be something devastating like assault or accidental death. Parents understand the impact of their children becoming adults and being on their own for the first time. However, parents should encourage constant communication with their children. They should try to be aware of the issues their children are facing. Try and learn about their closest friends at school, and make sure they are being as safe as they can. There is no way to protect your children from all the dangers of the world, but you must prepare them to be responsible.

Worrisome peer pressure motives in high school are just the beginning. In college, many other factors come into play, and your children may not have someone to whom they can easily turn when they need a trusting shoulder. You should try to be that shoulder as much as possible. The ease of access to alcohol in college is alarming, but more important than that is our responsibility as parents to be there for our children to guide them through this time.

---

24. CDC, "Impaired Driving."
25. NIAAA, "Alcohol Facts and Statistics."

As indicated earlier, we must do everything in moderation. Studies show that moderate drinking can be beneficial. It can help eliminate diseases, reduce the risk of heart disease, burn fat, improve sexual desire in both men and women, provide healthy antioxidants, and cause women to live longer. To be clear, moderate drinking means one glass of wine for women and two for men. Keep in mind that overindulgence in alcoholic beverages has an adverse effect.

THE BIBLICAL DRINK AND ITS GUIDELINES

Before any of these studies were done, the Bible told stories where people were permitted to drink moderately. God instructed people to present a drink offering in Exodus 29:40, and he told his people to enjoy wine in Deuteronomy 14:26. God also mentioned using "wine to gladden the heart of man" (Psalm 104:15). Before our modern-day research, the Bible stated that wine is good for our hearts. This is in reference to wine made purely from the ingredients of the earth. However, when we start including additives and other chemicals in our drinks while consuming them with an overindulgence mindset, we cross God's intention. Luke 7:34 states Jesus himself was "eating and drinking." But we like to change the meaning of biblical Scripture to fit our self-serving purposes; thus we confuse drinking wine with a meal or having a glass of wine with drinking wine for gluttony's sake.

According to 1 Corinthians 11:17–34, people should not overindulge in food and drink. Our bodies inherently know when enough is enough, but we constantly overindulge. When we begin to become less lucid and less coherent, this is our body telling us to take it easy. It is telling us we have approached our limit of consumption, but we usually fail to adhere to our internal warning signs. I assume God knew when he made us that we would have to tendency to take a mile when he gave us an inch when it comes to drinking, so he warns us in Corinthians and adds internal humanistic alerts to impede our fleshly desires. First Peter 4:3 states we should not have an excess of wine. The verse also goes on to list a host of other things in which we should not overindulge. The guidelines have been set; it is up to us to follow them.

However, we usually have a difficult time adhering to these simple rules laid out plainly in the Bible We should not abuse God's blessing or what he has given us. Noah was a drunkard. Lot became drunk and it led to immorality. You will also find that Proverbs 20:1 speaks about wine, calling it a mocker. Too much wine makes you become less of who you are and influences your actions. That proverb also states that strong drink is raging and whosoever is deceived by it is not wise.

Let us not be deceived in thinking that we should drink to no end without consequences. There are always consequences to our actions. Proverbs 23:20–21 speaks explicitly about drinking and the results of becoming inebriated. It states, "Be not among drunkards or among gluttonous eaters of meat, for the drunkard and the glutton will come to poverty, and slumber will clothe them with rags." The power of Proverbs is exactly what we see today, showing that it speaks prophetically about the doldrums of alcoholism.

These two verses from Proverbs comprise the dismay of drinking and its implications of poverty, as well as how laziness supports these fruitless efforts.

You must take care to not be fooled regarding the idea of becoming a drunkard. Your intentions may be to have a good time, but your life is worth more than one drunken night out on the town. It is worth more than having a constant battle with an enemy who has no hands to strike you and no weapon to disable, yet to whom you are losing the battle at every turn. Proverbs 23 goes into more detail about the struggles of a drunkard, describing the anguish, complaining, unnecessary bruises, bloodshot eyes, hallucinating, saying crazy things, staggering, and getting into a fight with anyone without knowing anything about it.

Many people have either personally seen or know of someone who may be considered an alcoholic or likes to overindulge in alcoholic beverages. You may know someone who has experienced a similar situation to the one being described. Did you notice their bloodshot eyes? Do they spend long hours at the bars? Are they always fighting or complaining about something not being right in their lives? Do they say crazy things? Do they sway back and forth, staggering around as they walk? Have you seen them in a fight, completely unaware they are being beaten? You could probably pull up many videos on YouTube displaying many accounts of drunken fights. The Bible has already warned us of this behavior. Yet so many of us continue to ignore the apparent warnings and heed the advice of those telling us not to overindulge.

Proverbs 23:33 states, "Your eyes will see strange things, and your heart utter perverse things." I understand this passage as alcohol driving a person to lust, to say wicked or corrupt things, and to act out of character. Rape, abuse, and lack of self-control can be found in many cases where alcohol consumption was given as the reason for their actions.

As noted with college students, alcohol is a contributing factor in many sexual incidents on school campuses. We need to read our Bible to understand that most, if not all, the challenges we face have been discussed in the Bible—as well as the solutions to overcome them. America has a drinking problem simply because we have created a drinking problem in this country. We have a lack of restraint and control, which makes us go beyond what God intended, thus causing us to fail every time. We must change our paths to save ourselves, save our children, stop dying prematurely, and move toward God.

The Only Solution to the Seven Challenges We Face in America

The Only Way Forward Is through God

Each of the seven challenges has been discussed with reference to what the Bible has to say about such matters. I find it fascinating that more than two thousand years since Jesus's death, the words from the Bible still have relevance to the situations we are facing today. The more we evolve or devolve, depending on our perspective in life, the more we share similar stories and perhaps a similar fate to those who came before us.

I am not a saint. I have sinned and continue to fall short of God's perfect will daily, so I am not perfect. I am not killing, stealing, or committing adultery, but I continuously commit sins, as so many of us do. I fall short of the Lord's expectations. Anytime I do not listen to what the Lord has instructed me to do, I am sinning and falling short. It took being separated from a job that I knew did not fit my personality or my spiritual quest for God to finally do what the Lord had been instructing me to do all along. I still become discouraged and want to stop moving forward. I want to watch sports or find some other means of entertainment to distract me from God's ultimate purpose. But I know God is working through me at this moment.

When I started this book, I did not intend to use Bible references to buttress my arguments. I only intended to list the seven ways we die prematurely. I planned to provide insight as to how we deal with them as a nation, simply because I thought too many Americans were struggling with these prevalent challenges. However, the Bible references kept coming to me. I kept researching what God had to say about these issues. I wondered if biblical people and stories dealt with the issues we were facing or provided guidance as to how we could overcome the challenges that oppress us daily. I found great support in the Bible, from both the Old and New Testaments, discussing solutions for each of the seven challenges I mentioned. I also wanted to tell my story and my encounters with some of these challenges, as it felt disingenuous to discuss topics about which I knew nothing.

Every day, even when I was not writing, I felt like I was living a purpose-filled life, helping to advance the message of God. I felt in my heart that this was the beginning of the work that God wanted me to do. I needed to start talking about him more. I needed to begin helping and reaching out to people through the talents he has given me. I am not a preacher or a reverend. I do not seek acknowledgment or even fanfare. I only wish the best for us as a people and for us to begin to understand what we are doing to ourselves and the world, from corner to corner.

In my travels, or even just on a trip to the grocery store, I look at people and wonder if we know our purpose in life or if we are just living. We are not supposed to be just living. We are not supposed to be trapped by human or worldly things. We all have a mission here, and it is not our day jobs. It cannot be our jobs, when most of us do the same thing every day without making any purposeful progress. Your spirit begins to despise you for torturing it, especially when you are living life without trying to understand what it is that you are truly supposed to be doing.

There are plenty of people who know the Bible better than I, as this is my current educational session. But this book—although it quotes biblical references—was written by guided hands. I wrote it based on my faith and inspiration, nothing more. I am not the best writer, but I have developed a relationship with God that is more powerful than I could have ever imagined it would be—so here I am writing. This is how I am certain the seven challenges against which we are struggling are challenges we can overcome, because God has already told us how to manage them. It is up to us to remove our biases, remove our prejudice, remove our judgment, and remove our reluctance to do more than what is comfortable. We must also remove our interpretations or prejudices of one another, because God speaks to each of us differently, so we should not judge another person based on our limited knowledge.

Our understanding is nothing like that of God's. He has told us what to do to live a purposeful life. If we were to only do the basic principles of the Ten Commandments, the troubles of the world would change dramatically. However, our souls are so far removed from what would be considered basic that we completely disregard the will of the Lord and do things our distorted way.

What parent would be happy if the children completely disregarded the rules of the house, yet still lived under the parent's roof? This is how God feels about us. We are his children, yet we are not abiding by the rules of his house.

It does not matter what your religion is. It does not matter if you are one variety of the many Christian faiths, Muslim, Jewish, or whatever you want your religion to be. We all call on God as the highest of the high. Christians believe Jesus is the key, Muslims believe Muhammad is the one, and Jews believe in Abraham. Every dogmatic principality we adhere to has a bit of influence by man; therefore, it is inherently flawed to some extent. The appreciation for God is all there needs to be said. But we allow our tainted behaviors of being human to strain our relationships with one another to the extent that God—with all his forgiving glory—cannot be pleased with who we are today.

Unfortunately, our story has been written before. We can reference Sodom and Gomorrah or that biblical story about the time when the earth was flooded after raining forty days and forty nights. This is not the first time that people walked away from God, doing things according to their fleshly satisfaction. Those people paid for their transgressions; do we not think that our time will come as well?

Our lives are but a capsule, and these seven challenges speak to the essence of things we can change. Life presents us with options every day to become better people. We must not take for granted the trials that life takes us through. God uses these tests as opportunities to make us stronger. The strength we gain must be applied to our lives daily. I am not saying any of this is easy. Overcoming any test or challenge in life requires you giving more of yourself, dedicating yourself a little more, and always striving to persevere. Trust God to be with you every step of the way, and he will surely see you through.

WORK TO PLEASE GOD ONLY

There are some instances where we cannot change some of the challenges we are facing, but we can most certainly create habits that alter our current path. For example, working ourselves to death is something we can change. There is no reason for us to be so busy that we are killing ourselves. Pastor Warren writes, "Being busy is a barrier to relationships."[1] This topic speaks to both working yourself to death and how we handle relationships. No matter how much money we have, some people are prone to working themselves tirelessly until the day that death arises.

The Bible states that we are to work six days, and that is all. Jesus flexed the Sabbath a little by doing works on the sanctified day but providing an explanation that makes sense. If my children or dog were in trouble on the

---

1. Warren, *Purpose Driven Life*, 21.

Sabbath, would I not work to save them? My answer is yes. I would work on the Sabbath to save my children. However, religions have now taken what is deemed the Sabbath day and changed it to apply to the day that best suits them. A lot of Christians worship on Sunday and deem it to be their Sabbath. Other sects of Christianity like the Seventh-Day Adventists hold their Sabbath on Saturday. I recall one Christian pastor stating that he works on Sunday since preaching is his job; therefore, Monday is his Sabbath. If you were a layman unfamiliar with the guidelines surrounding the holy day, how would you know which day the Sabbath is?

The Bible does not list days in the way that we know of them today. For example, the Bible describes timeframes or settings like the first month and tenth day or the eleventh month and ninth day. The fact that God created the world in six days and rested on the seventh is still being interpreted as to when is the actual Sabbath. Over one hundred languages on Earth use the word Sabbath for Saturday. For example, the Spanish word for Saturday is Sabado, meaning Sabbath.

The Sabbath is Saturday, but the point I am trying to make is a blunt request for you to take a day of rest. You can count seven days from day one and discuss it with God about what you should do. Whatever day you plan to make your Sabbath, take a rest. Working to death is never the answer. We miss our family events, we miss our children growing up, and we have marriages that fall apart all because of work. Why are we working so hard? So the company you are working for can let you go when they miss next quarter's numbers and you suddenly become their most dispensable employee?

Perhaps you pull extra hours and extra tasks only to miss out on a bonus that has been promised to you. Professional sports have coaches who pour themselves into their jobs, only to be let go when their starting quarterback or point guard gets hurt and they have a bad season. They miss out on so much of their lives at home, only to lose the job two seasons later. We must adhere to God's words as they have been laid out before us, since working nonstop is not healthy for you or your family.

Take the time to appreciate life, even if you love what you do. Take the time to appreciate your family and God. Decrease your stress, and you will live longer because of it. Follow God's law and take one day off from everything. If we must work, Hebrews 12:14–15 provides us some insight as to what we should all be working toward. These verses state that we should "strive for peace with everyone, and for the holiness without which no one will see the Lord. See to it that no one fails to obtain the grace of God; that no 'root of bitterness' springs up and causes trouble, and by it many become defiled." We should watch out for each other; work to know one another; and give our bodies, minds, and souls some rest as God intended.

REPLACE HAPPINESS WITH JOY

Residing in a state of unhappiness is never a place you should stay too long. Once you begin to accept God into your life, you will no longer seek happiness; you will be filled with joy. The great thing about joy is that it does not leave you based on circumstances or the day-to-day changes in your life. Philippians 4:7 states, "And the peace of God, which surpasses all understanding, will guard your hearts and your minds in Christ Jesus." This peace is an unbreakable peace. However, it is not something that just shows up, it is something that must be worked on. But once you attain peace in God, be assured that you always have access to that peace. You will begin to develop a relationship with God that will make you smile from ear to ear. You will be one of those people you probably despise who has a smile on their face for no apparent reason.

However, it will be apparent to you that your happiness is no longer reliant upon the things of this world. Instead, your happiness will be grounded in all the things of God. Psalm 37:4 sums up the idea of replacing happiness with joy by stating, "Delight yourself in the LORD, and he will give you the desires of your heart." What more can you ask?

STRESS NO MORE

The solution to stress is simple to say but harder to do: let go and let God. It takes a great deal of practice and effort to completely surrender yourself and your worries to God. But when it comes to managing stress, we are called to do this one thing: trust in the Lord, casting all our worries and doubts upon him. If we do this, I am sure he will see you through.

There is no burden too big for God to handle and no worry too small. If something is bothering his children, God wants to know about it. Psalm 46:1 states "God is our refuge and strength, a very present help in trouble." Therefore, we can take comfort in knowing that we do not need to stress about anything. God is there to support us and help us get through anything we may be facing.

Do not stress about your job, your children, your marriage, your finances, your friends, your health, or any other challenge this world throws at you. If you are worrying, then you are eliminating the need to trust God. If you are worried, then you are negating the power of prayer. Cast your fears aside after you pray to God about whatever is troubling you and move by faith. Trust that God has your best interest in his heart. Sometimes you have to wait on God, because the path he wants you to take may have already been cleared. Just make sure not to worry while you wait, because as worry creeps in, faith creeps out.

You need faith to have a relationship with God. Nothing else will do. Faith will instill trust that will eliminate your stress. There is a biblical saying that "faith apart from works is dead" (James 2:26). Having faith that something will happen is not enough. You must do something for your faith to be fulfilled or to meet your goal. Once you set your mind to eliminating stress and stressful behaviors, you can then move by faith. Stress bars you in; faith sets you free. Place your fears and your stressors in the hands of God. He can move mountains for you in every aspect of your life and with every trial you face.

LET US MOVE FOR GOD

Laziness is a slap in the face to God, the God who has explicitly told us to work. I have already listed some Scriptures related to laziness. However, have you ever noticed laziness stealing away at your soul? Our bodies are made to move and to work. Do not allow being lazy to take anything away from you.

The brain wants to grow and be used more as well. The more the brain works, the less likely you are to develop dementia. Your entire body is naturally inclined to work. I have watched Jane Fonda and Lily Tomlin on their Netflix hit show *Grace and Frankie*, amazed at how put together these two seventy-year-old ladies are. As I mentioned, Ernestine Shephard is an incredible specimen who still works out even over the age of eighty, and she started working out at fifty-six. Therefore, it is never too late to get started being healthier and making healthier choices and to stop allowing laziness to overtake our lives. It is a commitment to change your behavior.

There is a mandate for our bodies to work and exercise. Psalm 19 mentions that God reveals himself to the world by his work. We have the same responsibility. We must work as creations of God. Our work will be how we are revealed to the world. When the Bible first introduces us to God, it mentions that he works. Who are we to not do as God did? Are we better than God? Colossians 3:23–24 states, "Whatever you do, work heartily, as for the Lord and not for men, knowing that from the Lord you will receive the inheritance as your reward. You are serving the Lord Christ."

Do not allow laziness to overtake any part of your life or your decision-making. Relationships, food choices, activity, and technology can all be used to help us be better people if we do not take the lazy approach. It is the Lord we are serving. Whatever we are doing, we should do our best at that task. We should align ourselves with the direction that God has for us. Do not seek earthly rewards as if this is all there is to life. Your earthly rewards are limited. But if we live and move as the Lord says move, then when the Lord says move, we will witness doors opening. We will flourish in the possibilities of being a child of God.

GOD WILL GIVE YOU ALL OF YOUR HEART'S DESIRES

Chasing money for the sake of chasing money is a foolish thing. We have heard many stories of people who gained enormous amounts of wealth only to lose it later. There are numerous stories of lottery winners who lost all they had won due to some unfortunate circumstances. God does not care about our money, fame, or fortune. The Bible states that the meek will inherit the earth; it does not say the rich or the boastful will. Therefore, if you are lucky enough to be wealthy and have money, please take care to be humble about it. Make sure you always give back to those that are in need. It is easy for people to become lost amid financial gain. However, we must be cautious in our quest to earn more income. Ensure that our increase is attributed to—and in alignment with—God's desires for our financial well-being. Proverbs 23:4–5 states, "Do not toil to acquire wealth; be discerning enough to desist. When your eyes light on it, it is gone, for suddenly it sprouts wings, flying like an eagle toward heaven." Situations similar to what is being described in this verse happen all too often for us to not believe in the power of these words.

We think that all is well if we receive a windfall of money, but we should be careful and learn how to preserve that money. You should not run yourself into the ground chasing money. You should not wear yourself out trying to get rich, for money is often in one hand and out the other. Money is not here to stay and usually will leave as soon as it shows up, especially if you do not have a plan in place and God at the helm.

Hebrews 13:5 says, "Keep your life free from love of money, and be content with what you have." As you gain wealth, do not become married to it. Marry yourself to a relationship with God and work diligently serving his purpose for your life. Money loves no one. It is not faithful, which explains why it is elusive and disappears so many times. You earn money only to spend it on bills, taxes, or some unnecessary want or an actual need. I cannot tell you how many times we had some increase in income only to have some item break in the house or have car repair issues. I know we are not alone in dealing with unfortunate circumstances like these. They have happened to most of us.

If we love and care for one another, the opportunity to make money will present itself as well. Facebook is based on the premise of connecting people; now it is a billion-dollar organization. Their business model is that simple, because our love and interest in one another is a commodity. God knew this well before any company could profit from our togetherness. Facebook and other social platforms are capitalizing on our love and adoration, which is something God wants for everyone. Unlike social media platforms, there are no strings attached to caring for one another.

However, if you love money more than each other, you will slight one another just to be closer to money, when money is nothing more than a disloyal companion. Again, you can look at Facebook's struggles with allowing data to be shared with another company for financial gain during the 2016 election, having only to revert to its original purpose of sharing and connecting with one another. The fascination with money is not all it is cracked up to be.

LOVE ONE ANOTHER AS GOD LOVES US ALL

The selfish nature of man has always been his downfall. It is difficult not to be selfish, since self-preservation is innate. It is also something that we understand at a young age. However, when we live by the guidelines of a spiritual life that tell us to love each other and take care of one another, being selfish is quite contradictory. Many people and organizations are selfish. Some organizations and industries are designed to take from the poor, although we all have a biblical mandate to look after the poor. Some people are not willing to part with their money, time, or love for philanthropic, generous, or caring initiatives. We must be aware of who we are in this world and give as much of ourselves as we can to helping each other.

God's solution for selfishness is loving one another like a family. Throughout time, he has urged humanity to be more lenient and become more caring. Jesus died on the cross for the sake of love. God loved us so much that he gave his only begotten son. This story has been told across the world to Christians and non-Christians alike. To love one another does not mean you need to have a religious preference. It only takes compassion and a bit of humanity.

Moses was guided by God to free all the Israelites from Egypt. Although Moses did not think he was qualified to save an entire race of people, it was his selfless act that allowed millions of Israelites to be freed from the shackles of slavery. There are countless acts of removing selfishness from the equation for the greater good of mankind. Our lives are no different.

We are also called not to be selfish but to give without the desire of wanting anything in return. Altruism should be the societal governance of America, but in a country where capitalism reigns supreme, overcoming selfishness will take an unfathomable love akin to the agape love that God provides. It is a love we must pursue.

OVERINDULGE IN GOD'S LOVE

I once had a conversation with my wife regarding inhibitions and their purpose. We are born with natural inhibitions that are lowered when we overindulge in worldly activities. When we are under the influence of sexual desire, alcohol, drugs, or some other foreign substance that overtakes our bodies, we are prone to not behaving in a godly manner. We make decisions that can destroy our lives in a matter of minutes. These inhibitions are there to make sure we do not drink this or smoke that. They tell us we should not sleep with that person or this person. However, we choose to ignore these warnings to show that we are in control or to fulfill a secular conquest.

Often, we become victims of circumstance. Children are born out of wedlock, people are killed by drunk drivers, an STD or STI is passed from one person to the next. We like to believe we are free in the world. Yes, God has provided us with the freedom to do what we choose; however, all our decisions have consequences. We need to have restraint in what we should and should not do. First Corinthians 6:19–20 states, "Do you not know that your body is a temple of the Holy Spirit within you, whom you have from God? You are not your own, for you were bought with a price. So glorify God in your body." We must control ourselves and submit to the will of God. Sometimes we are not able to do it by ourselves; therefore, we must call on God and ask for help. His help is all that we need. Refrain from worldly desires that pit us against his love. Instead, indulge in all that God has for you.

GOD IS THE ONLY ANSWER

The seven challenges discussed in this book are tied to each other. Working to death can spur on being unhappy, while ruining relationships through an endless pursuit of chasing money results in you being selfish. Unhappiness and selfishness culminate in stress, which does not allow you time to rest. Not resting can make you lazy in other aspects of your life, thus leading to an overindulgence of poor habits like drinking to comfort you from all the things that may be getting you down.

The ultimate solution to all your troubles is developing a relationship with God. There is no other alternative that I have found. There are manmade options to deal with some of these seven challenges. But until we figure out what is wrong with us personally, it will be difficult to use only a manmade option as a complete solution. We should inquire about God, seek his guidance, and move forward with his love. This is the only way we can repair the foundation of America. This is the only way we can improve upon our history for a better tomorrow.

In all that we do, place God first and trust in him to aid us when we are living through human fallacies. Second Peter 1:3–4 states:

> His divine power has granted to us all things that pertain to life and godliness, through the knowledge of him who called us to his own glory and excellence, by which he has granted to us his precious and very great promises, so that through them you may become partakers of the divine nature, having escaped from the corruption that is in the world because of sinful desire.

So much of our downfall before these challenges lies solely at the hands of human desire. We must break the chain of human ambition that lacks the spirit of God. Human behavior without God lends itself to evil. As 1 Peter 2:1–2 says, "So put away all malice and all deceit and hypocrisy and envy and all slander. Like newborn infants, long for the pure spiritual milk, that by it you may grow up into salvation."

Have you cried out to God for nourishment? Today, you need God to nourish your spirit and provide you with a breakthrough beyond measure. These seven challenges appear primarily due to an absence of God. For if we loved God and appreciated his presence, we would not rob the poor and less fortunate but instead give food to the hungry and provide clothes for the needy. We would not be led by our ambitions and reckless desires that do not coincide with the purpose of God. We would not allow these seven challenges to rule our lives; instead, we would place all our worry, doubt, and problems at the feet of God. America would be better for it, the world would be better for it, and, most of all, you would be better for it. Love one another with the love of God. This is our mandate, and we have only one solution for all that troubles us: God.

The only solution is God.
Not your God, not his God, not my God—
just God, plain and simple.
The solution has been here the whole time . . .
God!

Lord, have mercy upon us and grant us an opportunity to make it right in your eyes, for we know not what we do or the magnitude of our actions. As sinners, we fall short. But I ask for your love to be unwavering and your forgiveness to be ever-enduring. As humans, we have never been able to live up to your expectations, which are simple and timeless; we lack the courage to always do what is right.

Keep us, protect us, and show us how to love, Father, now and forever.

Bibliography

Adams, Susan. "Most Americans Are Unhappy at Work." http://www.forbes.com/sites/susanadams/2014/06/20/most-americans-are-unhappy-at-work/#45dbbb6e5862.
Addictivelists.com. "Religious Wars." Site discontinued.
American Institute of Stress. "What Is Stress?" http://www.stress.org/what-is-stress/.
American Psychiatric Association. "What Is Depression?" https://www.psychiatry.org/patients-families/depression/what-is-depression.
American Sexual Health Association. "STDs: A to Z." https://www.ashasexualhealth.org/stds_a_to_z/.
Bello, Marisol, and Meghan Hoyer "Parents Who Do the Unthinkable—Kill Their Children." *USA Today,* Sept. 10, 2014. http://www.usatoday.com/story/news/nation/2014/09/10/parents-kill-children-fbi-data/15280259/.
BibleStudy.org. "What Is Defiling the Marriage Bed?" http://www.Biblestudy.org/question/what-is-defiling-the-marriage-bed.html.
Braaten, Kari P., and Marc R. Laufer. "Human Papillomavirus (HPV), HPV-Related Disease, and the HPV Vaccine." https://www.ncbi.nlm.nih.gov/pmc/articles/PMC2492590/#B1.
Bullying Statistics. "Bullying and Suicide." http://www.bullyingstatistics.org/content/bullying-and-suicide.html.
Carter, Shawn, and J. Smith. "Meet the Parents." New York: Universal, 2002.
Centers for Disease Control and Prevention. "Impaired Driving: Get the Facts." https://www.cdc.gov/transportationsafety/impaired_driving/impaired-drv_factsheet.html.
———. "National Health and Nutrition Examination Survey." https://www.cdc.gov/nchs/nhanes/index.htm.
———. "The Relationship between Bullying and Suicide: What We Know and What It Means for Schools." https://www.cdc.gov/violenceprevention/pdf/bullying-suicide-translation-final-a.pdf.
———. "Sexually Transmitted Disease Surveillance, 2011." http://www.cdc.gov/std/stats11/Surv2011.pdf.
———. "Stress . . . at Work." https://www.cdc.gov/niosh/docs/99-101/.
Chery, Fritz. "Idle Hands." http://Biblereasons.com/idle-hands/.

Cole, Jermaine. "Love Yourz." New York: Columbia, 2016.
———. "She's Mine Pt. 2." Santa Monica, CA: Universal, 2016.
Crigger, Megan, and Laura Santhanam. "How Many Americans Have Died in U.S. Wars?" PBS News Hour, May 24, 2015; updated on May 27, 2019. https://www.pbs.org/newshour/nation/many-americans-died-u-s-wars.
Crossway Bibles. "One Hundred Bible Verses about Stress." https://www.openBible.info/topics/stress.
———. "One Hundred Bible Verses about Happiness." https://www.openBible.info/topics/happiness.
DeFrank, Polly, and Mike Brunker. "Since Sandy Hook, an American Kid Has Died by a Gun Every Other Day." NBC News, Dec. 14, 2015. http://www.nbcnews.com/news/us-news/sandy-hook-american-kid-has-died-gun-every-other-day-n478746.
DoSomething.org. "Eleven Facts about World Hunger." https://www.dosomething.org/us/facts/11-facts-about-world-hunger.
Eichelberger, Erika. "Violence on the Home Front." Mother Jones, Apr. 25, 2013. http://m.motherjones.com/politics/2013/04/domestic-violence-murder-stats.
Eric. "Eleven Common Traits of Mass Murderers and Serial Killers." AvvoStories, Mar. 4, 2011. http://stories.avvo.com/crime/murder/11-common-traits-of-mass-murderers-and-serial-killers.html.
Fieldstadt, Elisha. "Georgia Dad Charged in Hot Car Deaths of Twin Toddlers." NBC News, Aug. 5, 2016. http://www.nbcnews.com/news/us-news/georgia-dad-charged-hot-car-deaths-twin-toddlers-n624046.
Fottrell, Quentin. "Five Reasons Americans Are Unhappy." MarketWatch, Aug. 30, 2014. https://www.marketwatch.com/story/5-reasons-americans-are-unhappy-2014-08-19.
Giokaris, John. "Twenty Ridiculous Ways the Government Wasted Your Money in 2013." Mic, Dec. 19, 2013. https://www.mic.com/articles/76985/20-ridiculous-ways-the-government-wasted-your-money-in-2013.
Gray, F. Gary, dir. *Friday*. Burbank, CA: New Line, 1995.
Griffin, R. Morgan. "Ten Health Problems Related to Stress That You Can Fix." WebMD, Apr. 1, 2014. http://www.webmd.com/balance/stress-management/features/10-fixable-stress-related-health-problems.
Gun Violence Archive. "About." https://www.gunviolencearchive.org/about.
Hartz-Seeley, Deborah S. "Chronic Stress Is Linked to the Six Leading Causes of Death." *Miami Herald*, Mar. 21, 2014. http://www.miamiherald.com/living/article1961770.html.
Hybels, Bill. *Honest to God?: Becoming an Authentic Christian*. Grand Rapids: Zondervan, 1992.
Washington's Blog and Global Research. "America Has Been at War 93 Percent of the Time—222 Out of 239 Years—Since 1776." GlobalResearch, Feb. 20, 2015. https://www.globalresearch.ca/america-has-been-at-war-93-of-the-time-222-out-of-239-years-since-1776/5565946.
International Overdose Awareness Day. "Facts and Stats." http://www.overdoseday.com/resources/facts-stats/.
Jakes, T. D. *The Ten Commandments of Working in a Hostile Environment*. New York: Berkley, 2005.
Johannsen, Cryn. "The Ones We've Lost: The Student Loan Debt Suicides." HuffPost, July 2, 2012. https://www.huffpost.com/entry/student-loan-debt-suicides_b_1638972.

Johnson, Angela. "Seventy-Six Percent of Americans are Living Paycheck-to-Paycheck." CNN Money, June 24, 2013. http://money.cnn.com/2013/06/24/pf/emergency-savings/.

Johnson, Jeffrey A., Sr. *The Song of Solomon: Love, Sex, and Relationships.* Maitland, FL: Xulon Press, 2007.

Koskie, Brandi. "Depression: Facts, Statistics, and You." http://www.healthline.com/health/depression/statistics-infographic.

Kurani, Nisha, et al. "How Does the Quality of the U.S. Healthcare System Compare to Other Countries?" https://www.healthsystemtracker.org/chart-collection/quality-u-s-healthcare-system-compare-countries/.

LaMotte, Sandee. "Celebrities Who Died from Painkillers, Cocaine and Heroin." CNN Health, updated Apr. 25, 2017. http://www.cnn.com/2016/06/03/health/gallery/celebrities-who-died-from-opioids/.

Levin, Jack, and James Fox. *Extreme Killing: Understanding Serial and Mass Murder.* Thousand Oaks, CA: Sage, 2005.

Levintova, Hannah. "Is Giving Food to the Homeless Illegal in Your City Too?" Mother Jones, Nov. 13, 2014. http://www.motherjones.com/politics/2014/11/90-year-old-florida-veteran-arrested-feeding-homeless-bans.

Livingston, Gretchen. "Fewer than Half of U.S. Kids Today Live in a 'Traditional' Family." Pew Research Center, Dec. 22, 2014. http://www.pewresearch.org/fact-tank/2014/12/22/less-than-half-of-u-s-kids-today-live-in-a-traditional-family/.

Madrid, Manuel. "With Hurricane Season Looming, Billions in Disaster Recovery for Puerto Rico Remain Unspent." American Prospect, Apr. 15, 2019. https://prospect.org/economy/hurricane-season-looming-billions-disaster-recovery-puerto-rico-remain-unspent/.

Mascia, Jennifer. "Fifteen Statistics That Tell the Story of Gun Violence This Year." Trace, Dec. 23, 2015. https://www.thetrace.org/2015/12/gun-violence-stats-2015/.

Mercola, Joseph. "One in Five American Deaths Now Associated with Obesity." http://articles.mercola.com/sites/articles/archive/2013/12/21/obesity-death-risk.aspx. Site discontinued.

Miller, Sara G. "The Deadliest Day of the Week." Live Science, Apr. 18, 2016. https://www.livescience.com/54429-deadliest-day-of-the-week.html.

Montaldo, Charles. "The Growing Problem of Road Rage." ThoughtCo., updated Apr. 10, 2017. https://web.archive.org/web/20171014120238/https://www.thoughtco.com/the-growing-problem-of-road-rage-973327.

Nati, Michelle. "Ten Older Women Who Look Decades Younger." Oddee, Nov. 20, 2014. http://www.oddee.com/item_99151.aspx.

National Alliance to End Homelessness. "Homelessness in America." http://www.endhomelessness.org/pages/snapshot_of_homelessness.

National Council on Alcoholism and Drug Dependence. "Facts about Alcohol." https://www.ncadd.org/about-addiction/alcohol/facts-about-alcohol.

National Institute of Mental Health "Major Depression." https://www.nimh.nih.gov/health/statistics/major-depression.

National Institute on Alcohol Abuse and Alcoholism. "Alcohol Facts and Statistics." https://www.niaaa.nih.gov/publications/brochures-and-fact-sheets/alcohol-facts-and-statistics.

National Health Care for the Homeless Council. "Fact Sheets." https://nhchc.org/wp-content/uploads/2020/12/Section-1-Toolkit.pdf.

National Institute of Diabetes and Digestive and Kidney Diseases. "Overweight and Obesity Statistics." https://www.niddk.nih.gov/health-information/health-statistics/overweight-obesity?dkrd=hispto880.

National Institute on Drug Abuse. "Trends and Statistics." https://www.drugabuse.gov/publications/drugfacts/nationwide-trends.

Nielsen Company. "Kids' Audience Behavior across Platforms." https://www.nielsen.com/wp-content/uploads/sites/3/2019/04/kids-audience-behavior-across-platforms-aug-2015.pdf.

Oberbrunner, Kary. "Six Warning Signs You Might be a Candidate for Karōshi (Death Caused by Your Day Job)." http://www.dayjobtodreamjob.com/6-warning-signs-you-might-be-a-candidate-for-karoshi-death-caused-by-your-day-job/.

Oldham, Abbey. "Two Thousand Fifteen: The Year of Mass Shootings." PBS News Hour, Jan. 1, 2016. https://www.pbs.org/newshour/nation/2015-the-year-of-mass-shootings.

Orwell, George. *Animal Farm*. New York: New American Library, 1946.

Petroff, Alanna. "Financial Crisis Caused 5000 Suicides." CNN Money, Sept. 18, 2013. http://money.cnn.com/2013/09/18/news/economy/financial-crisis-suicide/.

Pidgeon, Emily. "The Economic Impact of Bad Meetings." Ideas.TED.com, Nov. 17, 2014. https://ideas.ted.com/the-economic-impact-of-bad-meetings/.

Plourd, Kate. "Count 'Em: Sixty-Three CFOs Convicted in the Past Five Years." https://CFO, Aug. 3, 2007. www.cfo.com/risk-compliance/2007/08/count-em-63-cfos-convicted-in-past-five-years/

Plumer, Brad. "Only 27 Percent of College Grads Have a Job Related to Their Major." *Washington Post*, May 20, 2013. https://www.washingtonpost.com/news/wonk/wp/2013/05/20/only-27-percent-of-college-grads-have-a-job-related-to-their-major/.

Routhier, Sara. "Living on the Edge: Debts Increase Risk of Depression and Suicide." https://www.loans.org/personal/living-on-the-edge-debts-increase-risk-of-depression-and-suicide/.

Sandholtz, Nathan, et al. "Hate Crime Victimization, 2003–2011." http://www.bjs.gov/content/pub/pdf/hcv0311.pdf.

Sederer, Lloyd. "A Blind Eye to Addiction." US News, June 1, 2015. https://www.usnews.com/opinion/blogs/policy-dose/2015/06/01/america-is-neglecting-its-addiction-problem.

Single Mother Guide. "Single Mother Statistics." https://singlemotherguide.com/single-mother-statistics/.

Soleil, Gina. "Workplace Stress: The Health Epidemic of the Twenty-First Century." HuffPost, Jan. 7, 2016; updated Dec. 6, 2017. https://www.huffpost.com/entry/workplace-stress-the-heal_b_8923678.

Smith, Jeffrey. "Ten Reasons to Avoid GMOs." https://www.responsibletechnology.org/for-parents/parents-tool-kit/10-reasons-to-avoid-gmos/.

Somashekhar, Sandhya, and Steven Rich. "Final Tally: Police Shot and Killed 986 People in 2015." *Washington Post*, Jan. 6, 2016. https://www.washingtonpost.com/national/final-tally-police-shot-and-killed-984-people-in-2015/2016/01/05/3ec7a404-b3c5-11e5-a76a-0b5145e8679a_story.html.

Southern Poverty Law Center. "Active Hate Groups in the United States in 2015." https://www.splcenter.org/fighting-hate/intelligence-report/2016/active-hate-groups-united-states-2015.

Stoops, Michael, ed. "Food-Sharing Report: The Criminalization of Efforts to Feed People in Need." http://nationalhomeless.org/wp-content/uploads/2014/10/Food-Sharing2014.pdf.
Stopbullying.gov. "Effects of Bullying." http://www.stopbullying.gov/at-risk/effects/index.html#suicide.
Stump, Scott. "Adam Lanza's Father: I Wish He Had Never Been Born." Today, Mar. 10, 2014. https://www.today.com/news/adam-lanzas-father-i-wish-he-had-never-been-born-2D79346468.
Thiel, Peter, with Blake Masters. *Zero to One: Notes on Startups, or How to Build the Future*. New York: Crown Business, 2014.
Thompson, Derek. "Lotteries: America's $70 Billion Shame." *Atlantic*, May 11, 2015. https://www.theatlantic.com/business/archive/2015/05/lotteries-americas-70-billion-shame/392870/.
U.S. News. "Overall Best Countries Ranking." https://www.usnews.com/news/best-countries/overall-rankings.
Warren, Rick. *The Purpose Driven Life*. Grand Rapids: Zondervan, 2002.
Weinfield, Nancy S., et al. "Hunger in America 2014." http://help.feedingamerica.org/HungerInAmerica/hunger-in-america-2014-full-report.pdf.
West, Simon, dir. *Con Air*. Burbank, CA: Touchstone Pictures, 1997.
White, Stanley. "Death by Overwork on Rise among Japanese Vulnerable Workers." Reuters, Apr. 2, 2016. https://www.reuters.com/article/us-japan-economy-overwork/death-by-overwork-on-rise-among-japans-vulnerable-workers-idUSKCN0X000F.
World Health Organization. "WHO Publishes New Estimates on Congenital Syphilis." https://www.who.int/reproductivehealth/congenital-syphilis-estimates/en/.
YouVersion Bible App: Daily Study, Audio and Prayer. Edmond, OK: Life.Church, 2016. Mobile App. 9.0.6.

www.ingramcontent.com/pod-product-compliance
Lightning Source LLC
Chambersburg PA
CBHW050826160426
43192CB00010B/1913